Container Security
Fundamental Technology Concepts that Protect Containerized Applications

Liz Rice

Beijing · Boston · Farnham · Sebastopol · Tokyo

Container Security

by Liz Rice

Published by O'Reilly Media, Inc., 1005 Gravenstein Highway North, Sebastopol, CA 95472.

O'Reilly books may be purchased for educational, business, or sales promotional use. Online editions are also available for most titles (*http://oreilly.com*). For more information, contact our corporate/institutional sales department: 800-998-9938 or *corporate@oreilly.com*.

Acquisitions Editor: John Devins
Developmental Editor: Virginia Wilson
Production Editor: Nan Barber
Copyeditor: Arthur Johnson
Proofreader: Kim Wimpsett

Indexer: Devon Thomas
Interior Designer: David Futato
Cover Designer: Karen Montgomery
Illustrator: Rebecca Demarest

April 2020:   First Edition

Revision History for the First Edition
2020-04-03:   First Release

See *http://oreilly.com/catalog/errata.csp?isbn=9781492056706* for release details.

978-1-492-05670-6

[LSI]

Table of Contents

Preface

Many organizations are running applications in cloud native environments, using containers and orchestration to facilitate scalability and resilience. If you're a member of the Operations, the DevOps, or even the DevSecOps team setting up these environments for your company, how do you know whether your deployments are secure? If you're a security professional with experience in traditional server-based or virtual machine–based systems, how can you adapt your existing knowledge for container-based deployments? And as a developer in the cloud native world, what do you need to think about to improve the security of your containerized applications? This book delves into some of the key underlying technologies that containers and cloud native rely on, to leave you better equipped to assess the security risks and potential solutions applicable to your environment and to help you avoid falling into bad practices that will leave your technology deployments exposed.

In this book you will learn about many of the building block technologies and mechanisms that are commonly used in container-based systems, and how they are constructed in the Linux operating system. Together we will dive deep into the underpinnings of how containers work and how they communicate so that you are well versed not just in the "what" of container security but also, and more importantly, in the "why." My goal in writing this book is to help you better understand what's happening when you deploy containers. I want to encourage you to build mental models that allow you to make your own assessment of potential security risks that could affect your deployments.

This book primarily considers the kind of "application containers" that many businesses are using these days to run their business applications in systems such as Kubernetes and Docker. This is in contrast to "system containers" such as LXC and LXD from the Linux Containers Project (*https://linuxcontainers.org*). In an application container, you are encouraged to run immutable containers with as little code as is necessary to run the application, whereas in a system container environment the idea is to run an entire Linux distribution and treat it more like a virtual machine. It's considered perfectly normal to SSH into a system container, but application container security experts will look at you askance if you want to SSH into an application container (for reasons covered later in this book). However, the basic mechanisms used to create application and system containers alike are control groups, namespaces, and changing the root directory, so this book will give you a solid foundation from which you may wish to explore the differences in approach taken by the different container projects.

Who This Book Is For

Whether you consider yourself a developer, a security professional, an operator, or a manager, this book will suit you best if you like to get into the nitty-gritty of how things work, and if you enjoy time spent in a Linux terminal.

If you are looking for an instruction manual that gives a step-by-step guide to securing containers, this may not be the book for you. I don't believe there is a one-size-fits-all approach that would work for every application in every environment and every organization. Instead, I want to help you understand what is happening when you run applications in containers, and how different security mechanisms work, so that you can judge the risks for yourself.

As you'll find out later in this book, containers are made with a combination of features from the Linux kernel. Securing containers involves using a lot of the same mechanisms as you would use on a Linux host. (I use the term "host" to cover both virtual machines and bare-metal servers.) I lay out how these mechanisms work and then show how they apply in containers. If you are an experienced system administrator, you'll be able to skip over some sections to get to the container-specific information.

I assume that you have some basic familiarity with containers, and you have probably at least toyed with Docker or Kubernetes. You will understand terms like "pulling a container image from a registry" or "running a container" even if you don't know exactly what is happening under the covers when you take these actions. I don't expect you to know the details of how containers work—at least, not until you have read the book.

What This Book Covers

We'll start in Chapter 1 by considering threat models and attack vectors that affect container deployments, and the aspects that differentiate container security from traditional deployment security. The remainder of the book is concerned with helping you build a thorough understanding of containers and these container-specific threats, and with how you can defend against them.

Before you can really think about how to secure containers, you'll need to know how they work. Chapter 2 sets the scene by describing some core Linux mechanisms such as system calls and capabilities that will come into play when we use containers. Then in Chapters 3 and 4, we'll delve into the Linux constructs that containers are made from. This will give you an understanding of what containers really are and of the extent to which they are isolated from each other. We'll compare this with virtual machine isolation in Chapter 5.

In Chapter 6 you'll learn about the contents of container images and consider some best practices for building them securely. Chapter 7 addresses the need to identify container images with known software vulnerabilities.

In Chapter 8 we will look at some optional Linux security measures that can be applied to harden containers beyond the basic implementation we saw in Chapter 4. We will look into ways that container isolation can be compromised through dangerous but commonplace misconfigurations in Chapter 9.

Then we will turn to the communications between containers. Chapter 10 looks at how containers communicate and explores ways to leverage the connections between them to improve security. Chapter 11 explains the basics of keys and certificates, which containerized components can use to identify each other and set up secure network connections between themselves. This is no different for containers than it is for any other component, but this topic is included since keys and certificates are often a source of confusion in distributed systems. In Chapter 12 we will see how certificates and other credentials can be safely (or not so safely) passed to containers at runtime.

In Chapter 13 we will consider ways in which security tooling can prevent attacks at runtime, taking advantage of the features of containers.

Finally, Chapter 14 reviews the top 10 security risks published by the Open Web Application Security Project and considers container-specific approaches for addressing them. Spoiler alert: some of the top security risks are addressed in exactly the same way whether your application is containerized or not.

A Note about Kubernetes

These days the majority of folks using containers are doing so under the Kubernetes (*https://kubernetes.io*) orchestrator. An orchestrator automates the process of running different workloads in a cluster of machines, and there are places in this book where I will assume that you have a basic grasp of this concept. In general, I have tried to stay focused on concepts that act at the level of the underlying containers—the "data plane" in a Kubernetes deployment.

Because Kubernetes workloads run in containers, this book is relevant to Kubernetes security, but it is not a comprehensive treatment of everything related to securing Kubernetes or cloud native deployments. There are many other concerns around the configuration and use of the control plane components that are outside the scope of this book. If you would like more on this topic, you might be interested in the O'Reilly *Kubernetes Security* report (*https://oreil.ly/Of6yK*) (which I coauthored with Michael Hausenblas).

Examples

There are lots of examples in this book, and I encourage you to try them out for yourself.

In the examples I assume that you are comfortable with basic Linux command-line tools like ps and grep, and with the basic day-to-day activities of running container applications through the use of tools like kubectl or docker. This book will use the former set of tools to explain a lot more about what's happening when you use the latter!

To follow along with the examples in this book, you will need access to a Linux machine or virtual machine. I created the examples using an Ubuntu 19.04 virtual machine running under VirtualBox (*https://www.virtualbox.org/*) on my Mac; I also use Vagrant (*https://www.vagrantup.com/*) to create, start, and stop my virtual machines. You should be able to achieve similar results on different Linux distributions and using virtual machines from your favorite cloud provider.

How to Run Containers

For many people, their main (perhaps only) experience of running containers directly is with Docker. Docker democratized the use of containers by providing a set of tools that developers generally found easy to use. From a terminal, you manipulate containers and container images using the docker command.

This docker tool is really a thin layer making API calls to Docker's main component: a daemon that does all the hard work. Within the daemon is a component called containerd that is invoked whenever you want to run a container. The containerd component makes sure that the container image you want to run is in place, and it then calls a runc component to do the business of actually instantiating a container.

If you want to, you can run a container yourself by invoking containerd or even runc directly. The containerd project was donated by Docker to the Cloud Native Computing Foundation (*https://cncf.io*) (CNCF) back in 2017.

Kubernetes uses an interface called the Container Runtime Interface (CRI) beneath which users can opt for a container runtime of their choice. The most commonly used options today are the aforementioned `containerd` (*https://containerd.io*) and `CRI-O` (*https://cri-o.io*) (which originated from Red Hat before being donated to the CNCF).

The `docker` CLI is just one option for managing containers and images. There are several others you can use to run the kind of application containers covered in this book. Red Hat's `podman` tool, originally conceived to remove reliance on a daemon component, is one such option.

The examples in this book use a variety of different container tools to illustrate that there are multiple container implementations that share many common features.

Feedback

There is a website at *containersecurity.tech* to accompany this book. You are invited to raise issues there with feedback and any corrections that you'd like to see in future editions.

Conventions Used in This Book

The following typographical conventions are used in this book:

Italic
:   Indicates new terms, URLs, email addresses, filenames, and file extensions.

`Constant width`
:   Used for program listings, as well as within paragraphs to refer to program elements such as variable or function names, databases, data types, environment variables, statements, and keywords.

`Constant width bold`
:   Shows commands or other text that should be typed literally by the user.

`Constant width italic`
:   Shows text that should be replaced with user-supplied values or by values determined by context.

> This element signifies a general note.

Using Code Examples

Supplemental material (code examples, exercises, etc.) is available for download at *https://containersecurity.tech*.

If you have a technical question or a problem using the code examples, please send email to *bookquestions@oreilly.com*.

This book is here to help you get your job done. In general, if example code is offered with this book, you may use it in your programs and documentation. You do not need to contact us for permission unless you're reproducing a significant portion of the code. For example, writing a program that uses several chunks of code from this book does not require permission. Selling or distributing examples from O'Reilly books does require permission. Answering a question by citing this book and quoting example code does not require permission. Incorporating a significant amount of example code from this book into your product's documentation does require permission.

We appreciate, but generally do not require, attribution. An attribution usually includes the title, author, publisher, and ISBN. For example: "*Container Security* by Liz Rice (O'Reilly). Copyright 2020 Vertical Shift Ltd., 978-1-492-05670-6."

If you feel your use of code examples falls outside fair use or the permission given above, feel free to contact us at *permissions@oreilly.com*.

O'Reilly Online Learning

 For more than 40 years, *O'Reilly Media* has provided technology and business training, knowledge, and insight to help companies succeed.

Our unique network of experts and innovators share their knowledge and expertise through books, articles, and our online learning platform. O'Reilly's online learning platform gives you on-demand access to live training courses, in-depth learning paths, interactive coding environments, and a vast collection of text and video from O'Reilly and 200+ other publishers. For more information, please visit *http://oreilly.com*.

How to Contact Us

Please address comments and questions concerning this book to the publisher:

O'Reilly Media, Inc.
1005 Gravenstein Highway North

Sebastopol, CA 95472
800-998-9938 (in the United States or Canada)
707-829-0515 (international or local)
707-829-0104 (fax)

We have a web page for this book, where we list errata, examples, and any additional information. You can access this page at *https://oreil.ly/container-security*.

Email *bookquestions@oreilly.com* to comment or ask technical questions about this book.

For more information about our books, courses, and news, see our website at *http://www.oreilly.com*.

Find us on Facebook: *http://facebook.com/oreilly*

Follow us on Twitter: *http://twitter.com/oreillymedia*

Watch us on YouTube: *http://www.youtube.com/oreillymedia*

Acknowledgments

I'm grateful to many people who have helped and supported me through the process of writing this book.

- My editor at O'Reilly, Virginia Wilson, for keeping everything on track and making sure the book is up to scratch.
- The technical reviewers who provided thoughtful comments and actionable feedback: Akhil Behl, Alex Pollitt, Andrew Martin, Erik St. Martin, Phil Estes, Rani Osnat, and Robert P. J. Day.
- My colleagues at Aqua Security who taught me so much about container security over the years.
- Phil Pearl—my husband, my best critic and coach, and my best friend.

CHAPTER 1

Container Security Threats

In the last few years, the use of containers has exploded. The concepts around containers existed for several years before Docker, but most observers agree that it was Docker's easy-to-use command-line tools that started to popularize containers among the developer community from its launch in 2013.

Containers bring many advantages: as described in Docker's original tagline, they allow you to "build once, run anywhere." They do this by bundling together an application and all its dependencies and isolating the application from the rest of the machine it's running on. The containerized application has everything it needs, and it is easy to package up as a container image that will run the same on my laptop and yours, or in a server in a data center.

A knock-on effect of this isolation is that you can run multiple different containers side by side without them interfering with each other. Before containers, you could easily end up with a dependency nightmare where two applications required different versions of the same packages. The easiest solution to this problem was simply to run the applications on separate machines. With containers, the dependencies are isolated from each other so it becomes straightforward to run multiple apps on the same server. People quickly realized that they could take advantage of containerization to run multiple applications on the same host (whether it's a virtual machine or a bare-metal server) without having to worry about dependencies.

The next logical step was to spread containerized applications across a cluster of servers. Orchestrators such as Kubernetes automate this process so that you no longer have to manually install an app on a particular machine; you tell the orchestrator what containers you want to run, and it finds a suitable location for each one.

From a security perspective, many things are the same in a containerized environment as they are in a traditional deployment. There are attackers out in the world who want to steal data, or modify the way a system behaves, or use other people's compute resources to mine their own cryptocurrencies. This doesn't change when you move to containers. However, containers do change a lot about the way that applications run, and there are a different set of risks as a result.

Risks, Threats, and Mitigations

A *risk* is a potential problem, and the effects of that problem if it were to occur.

A *threat* is a path to that risk occurring.

A *mitigation* is a countermeasure against a threat—something you can do to prevent the threat or at least reduce the likelihood of its success.

For example, there is a risk that someone could steal your car keys from your house and thus drive off in your car. The threats would be the different ways they might steal the keys: breaking a window to reach in and pick them up; putting a fishing rod through your letter box; knocking on your door and distracting you while an accomplice slips in quickly to grab the keys. A mitigation for all these threats might be to keep your car keys out of sight.

Risks vary greatly from one organization to another. For a bank holding money on behalf of customers, the biggest risk is almost certainly that money being stolen. An ecommerce organization will worry about the risks of fraudulent transactions. An individual running a personal blog site might fear someone breaking in to impersonate them and post inappropriate comments. Because privacy regulations differ between nations, the risk of leaking customers' personal data varies with geography—in many countries the risk is "only" reputational, while in Europe the General Data Protection Regulation (GDPR) allows for fines of up to 4% of a company's total revenue (*https://oreil.ly/guQg3*).

Because the risks vary greatly, the relative importance of different threats will also vary, as will the appropriate set of mitigations. A risk management framework is a process for thinking about risks in a systematic way, enumerating the possible threats, prioritizing their importance, and defining an approach to mitigation.

Threat modeling is a process of identifying and enumerating the potential threats to a system. By systematically looking at the system's components and the possible modes of attack, a threat model can help you identify where your system is most vulnerable to attack.

There is no single comprehensive threat model, as it depends on your risks, your particular environment, your organization, and the applications you're running, but it is possible to list some potential threats that are common to most, if not all, container deployments.

Container Threat Model

One way to start thinking about the threat model is to consider the actors involved. These might include:

- *External attackers* attempting to access a deployment from outside
- *Internal attackers* who have managed to access some part of the deployment
- *Malicious internal actors* such as developers and administrators who have some level of privilege to access the deployment
- *Inadvertent internal actors* who may accidentally cause problems
- *Application processes* that, while not sentient beings intending to compromise your system, might have programmatic access to the system

Each actor has a certain set of permissions that you need to consider:

- What access do they have through credentials? For example, do they have access to user accounts on the host machines your deployment is running on?
- What permissions do they have on the system? In Kubernetes, this could refer to the role-based access control settings for each user, as well as anonymous users.
- What network access do they have? For example, which parts of the system are included within a Virtual Private Cloud (VPC)?

There are several possible routes to attacking a containerized deployment, and one way to map them is to think of the potential attack vectors at each stage of a container's life cycle. These are summarized in Figure 1-1.

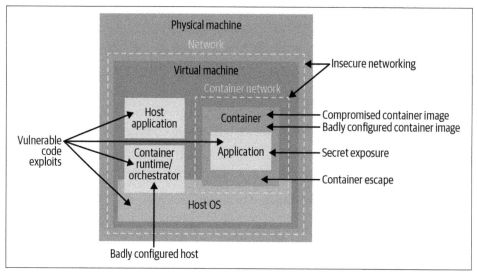

Figure 1-1. Container attack vectors

Vulnerable application code

> The life cycle starts with the application code that a developer writes. This code, and the third-party dependencies that it relies on, can include flaws known as vulnerabilities, and there are thousands of published vulnerabilities that an attacker can exploit if they are present in an application. The best way to avoid running containers with known vulnerabilities is to scan images, as you will see in Chapter 7. This isn't a one-off activity, because new vulnerabilities are discovered in existing code all the time. The scanning process also needs to identify when containers are running with out-of-date packages that need to be updated for security patches. Some scanners can also identify malware that has been built into an image.

Badly configured container images

> Once the code has been written, it gets built into a container image. When you are configuring how a container image is going to be built, there are plenty of opportunities to introduce weaknesses that can later be used to attack the running container. These include configuring the container to run as the root user, giving it more privilege on the host than it really needs. You'll read more about this in Chapter 6.

Build machine attacks

> If an attacker can modify or influence the way a container image is built, they could insert malicious code that will subsequently get run in the production environment. In addition, finding a foothold within the build environment could be a

stepping stone toward breaching the production environment. This is also discussed in Chapter 6.

Supply chain attacks

Once the container image is built, it gets stored in a registry, and it gets retrieved or "pulled" from the registry at the point where it's going to be run. How do you know that the image you pull is exactly the same as what you pushed earlier? Could it have been tampered with? An actor who can replace an image or modify an image between build and deployment has the ability to run arbitrary code on your deployment. This is another topic I'll cover in Chapter 6.

Badly configured containers

As we'll discuss in Chapter 9, it's possible to run containers with settings that give it unnecessary, and perhaps unplanned, privileges. If you download YAML configuration files from the internet, please don't run them without carefully checking that they do not include insecure settings!

Vulnerable hosts

Containers run on host machines, and you need to ensure that those hosts are not running vulnerable code (for example, old versions of orchestration components with known vulnerabilities). It's a good idea to minimize the amount of software installed on each host to reduce the attack surface, and hosts also need to be configured correctly according to security best practices. This is discussed in Chapter 4.

Exposed secrets

Application code often needs credentials, tokens, or passwords in order to communicate with other components in a system. In a containerized deployment, you need to be able to pass these secret values into the containerized code. As you'll see in Chapter 12, there are different approaches to this, with varying levels of security.

Insecure networking

Containers generally need to communicate with other containers or with the outside world. Chapter 10 discusses how networking works in containers, and Chapter 11 discusses setting up secure connections between components.

Container escape vulnerabilities

The widely used container runtimes including `containerd` and `CRI-O` are by now pretty battle-hardened, but it's still within the realm of possibility that there are bugs yet to be found that would let malicious code running inside a container escape out onto the host. One such issue, sometimes referred to as Runcescape (*https://oreil.ly/cFSaJ*), came to light as recently as 2019. You'll read about the isolation that is supposed to keep application code constrained within a container in Chapter 4. For some applications, the consequences of an escape could be sufficiently damaging that it's worth considering stronger isolation mechanisms, such as those covered in Chapter 8.

There are also some attack vectors that are outside the scope of this book.

- Source code is generally held in repositories, which could conceivably be attacked in order to poison the application. You will need to ensure that user access to the repository is controlled appropriately.

- Hosts are networked together, often using a VPC for security, and typically connected to the internet. Exactly as in a traditional deployment, you need to protect the host machines (or virtual machines) from access by threat actors. Secure network configuration, firewalling, and identity and access management all still apply in a cloud native deployment as they do in a traditional deployment.

- Containers typically run under an orchestrator—commonly Kubernetes in today's deployments, though there are other options such as Docker Swarm or Hashicorp Nomad. If the orchestrator is configured insecurely or if administrative access is not controlled effectively, this gives attackers additional vectors to affect the deployment.

> For more on threat models in Kubernetes deployments, you may be interested in reading the Kubernetes Threat Model (*https://oreil.ly/r0ZAG*) commissioned by the CNCF.
>
> In addition, the CNCF's Financial User Group has published a Kubernetes Attack Tree (*https://oreil.ly/r1lg8*) created using the STRIDE (*https://oreil.ly/rNmPN*) methodology.

Security Boundaries

A security boundary (sometimes called a trust boundary) appears between parts of the system, such that you would need some different set of permissions to move between those parts. Sometimes these boundaries are set up administratively—for example, in a Linux system, the system administrator can modify the security boundary defining what files a user can access by changing the groups that the user is a member of. If you are rusty on Linux file permissions, a refresher is coming up in Chapter 2.

A container is a security boundary. Application code is supposed to run within that container, and it should not be able to access code or data outside of the container except where it has explicitly been given permission to do so (for example, through a volume mounted into the container).

The more security boundaries there are between an attacker and their target (your customer data, for example), the harder it is for them to reach that target.

The attack vectors described in "Container Threat Model" on page 3 can be chained together to breach several security boundaries. For example:

- An attacker may find that because of a vulnerability in an application dependency, they are able to execute code remotely within a container.

- Suppose that the breached container doesn't have direct access to any data of value. The attacker needs to find a way to move out of the container, either to another container or to the host. A container escape vulnerability would be one route out of the container; insecure configuration of that container could provide another. If the attacker finds either of these routes available, they can now access the host.

- The next step would be to look for ways to gain root privileges on the host. This step might be trivial if your application code is running as root inside the container, as you'll see in Chapter 4.

- With root privileges on the host machine, the attacker can get to anything that the host, or any of the containers running on that host, can reach.

Adding and strengthening the security boundaries in your deployment will make life more difficult for the attacker.

An important aspect of the threat model is to consider the possibility of attacks from within the environment in which your applications are running. In cloud deployments, you may be sharing some resources with other users and their applications. Sharing machine resources is called *multitenancy*, and it has a significant bearing on the threat model.

Multitenancy

In a multitenant environment, different users, or *tenants*, run their workloads on shared hardware. (You may also come across the term "multitenancy" in a software application context, where it refers to multiple users sharing the same instance of software, but for the purposes of this discussion, only the hardware is shared.) Depending on who owns those different workloads and how much the different tenants trust each other, you might need stronger boundaries between them to prevent them from interfering with each other.

Multitenancy is a concept that has been around since the mainframe days in the 1960s, when customers rented CPU time, memory, and storage on a shared machine. This is not so very different from today's public clouds, like Amazon AWS, Microsoft Azure, and Google Cloud Platform, where customers rent CPU time, memory, and storage, along with other features and managed services. Since Amazon AWS launched EC2 back in 2006, we have been able to rent virtual machine instances running on racks of servers in data centers around the world. There may be many virtual machines (VMs) running on a physical machine, and as a cloud customer operating a set of VMs you have no idea who is operating the VMs that neighbor yours.

Shared Machines

There are situations in which a single Linux machine (or virtual machine) may be shared by many users. This is very common in university settings, for instance, and this is a good example of true multitenancy, where users don't trust each other and, quite frankly, the system administrators don't trust the users. In this environment Linux access controls are used to strictly limit user access. Each user has their own login ID, and the access controls of Linux are used to limit access to ensure, for example, that users can modify only files in their own directories. Can you imagine the chaos if university students could read, or—even worse—modify, their classmates' files?

As you'll see in Chapter 4, all the containers running on the same host share the same kernel. If the machine is running the Docker daemon, any user who can issue docker commands effectively has root access, so a system administrator won't want to grant that to untrusted users.

In enterprise situations, and more specifically in cloud native environments, you are less likely to see this kind of shared machine. Instead, users (or teams of users who trust each other) will typically use their own resources allocated to them in the form of virtual machines.

Virtualization

Generally speaking, virtual machines are considered to be pretty strongly isolated from each other, by which we mean that it's unlikely that your neighbors can observe or interfere with the activities in your VMs. You can read more about how this isolation is achieved in Chapter 5. In fact, according to the accepted definition (*https://oreil.ly/yfkQI*), virtualization doesn't count as multitenancy at all: multitenancy is when different groups of people share a single instance of the same software, and in virtualization the users don't have access to the hypervisor that manages their virtual machines, so they don't share any software.

That's not to say that the isolation between virtual machines is perfect, and historically users have complained about "noisy neighbor" issues, where the fact that you are sharing a physical machine with other users can result in unexpected variances in performance. Netflix was an early adopter of the public cloud, and in the section "Co-tenancy is hard" (*https://oreil.ly/CGlZ0*) in a 2010 blog post, it acknowledged that it built systems that might deliberately abandon a subtask if it proved to be operating too slowly. More recently, others have claimed that the noisy neighbor problem isn't a real issue (*https://oreil.ly/iE4qE*).

There have also been cases of software vulnerabilities that could compromise the boundary between virtual machines.

For some applications and some organizations (especially government, financial, or healthcare), the consequences of a security breach are sufficiently serious to warrant full physical separation. You can operate a private cloud, running in your own data center or managed by a service provider on your behalf, to ensure total isolation of your workloads. Private clouds sometimes come with additional security features such as additional background checks on the personnel who have access to the data center.

Many cloud providers have VM options where you are guaranteed to be the only customer on a physical machine. It's also possible to rent bare-metal machines operated by cloud providers. In both these scenarios, you will completely avoid the noisy neighbor issue, and you also have the advantage of the stronger security isolation between physical machines.

Whether you are renting physical or virtual machines in the cloud or using your own servers, if you're running containers, you may need to consider the security boundaries between multiple groups of users.

Container Multitenancy

As you'll see in Chapter 4, the isolation between containers is not as strong as that between VMs. While it does depend on your risk profile, it's unlikely that you want to use containers on the same machine as a party that you don't trust.

Even if all the containers running on your machines are run by you or by people you absolutely trust, you might still want to mitigate against the fallibility of humans by making sure that your containers can't interfere with each other.

In Kubernetes, you can use *namespaces* to subdivide a cluster of machines for use by different individuals, teams, or applications.

The word "namespace" is an overloaded term. In Kubernetes, a namespace is a high-level abstraction that subdivides cluster resources that can have different Kubernetes access controls applied to them. In Linux, a namespace is a low-level mechanism for isolating the machine resources that a process is aware of. You'll learn about this kind of namespace in detail in Chapter 4.

Use role-based access control (RBAC) to limit the people and components that can access these different Kubernetes namespaces. The details of how to do this are outside the scope of this book, but I would like to mention that Kubernetes RBAC controls only the actions you can perform through the Kubernetes API. Application containers in Kubernetes pods that happen to be running on the same host are protected from each other only by container isolation, as described in this book, even if they are in different namespaces. If an attacker can escape a container to the host, the Kubernetes namespace boundary makes not one jot of difference to their ability to affect other containers.

Container Instances

Cloud services such as Amazon AWS, Microsoft Azure, or Google Cloud Platform offer many *managed services*, through which the user can rent software, storage, and other components without having to install or manage them. A classic example is Amazon's Relational Database Service (RDS); with RDS, you can easily provision databases that use well-known software like PostgreSQL, and getting your data backed up is as simple as ticking a box (and paying a bill, of course).

Managed services have extended to the world of containers, too. Azure Container Instances and AWS Fargate are services that allow you to run containers without having to worry about the underlying machine (or virtual machine) on which they run.

This can save you from a significant management burden and allows you to easily scale the deployment at will. However, at least in theory, your container instances could be colocated on the same virtual machine as those of other customers. Check with your cloud provider if in doubt.

You are now aware of a good number of potential threats to your deployment. Before we dive into the rest of the book, I'd like to introduce some basic security principles that should guide your thinking when assessing what security tools and processes you need to introduce into your deployment.

Security Principles

These are general guidelines that are commonly considered to be a wise approach regardless of the details of what you're trying to secure.

Least Privilege

The principle of least privilege states that you should limit access to the bare minimum that a person or component needs in order to do their job. For example, if you have a microservice that performs product search in an ecommerce application, the principle of least privilege suggests that the microservice should only have credentials that give it read-only access to the product database. It has no need to access, say, user or payment information, and it has no need to write product information.

Defense in Depth

As you'll see in this book, there are many different ways you can improve the security of your deployment and the applications running within it. The principle of defense in depth tells us that you should apply layers of protection. If an attacker is able to breach one defense, another layer should prevent them from harming your deployment or exfiltrating your data.

Reducing the Attack Surface

As a general rule, the more complex a system is, the more likely it is that there is a way to attack it. Eliminating complexity can make the system harder to attack. This includes:

- Reducing access points by keeping interfaces small and simple where possible
- Limiting the users and components who can access a service
- Minimizing the amount of code

Limiting the Blast Radius

The concept of segmenting security controls into smaller subcomponents or "cells" means that should the worst happen, the impact is limited. Containers are well-suited to this principle, because by dividing an architecture into many instances of a microservice, the container itself can act as a security boundary.

Segregation of Duties

Related to both least privilege and limiting blast radius is the idea of segregating duties so that, as much as possible, different components or people are given authority over only the smallest subset of the overall system that they need. This approach limits the damage a single privileged user might inflict by ensuring that certain operations require more than one user's authority.

Applying Security Principles with Containers

As you'll see in later sections of this book, the granularity of containers can help us in the application of all these security principles.

Least privilege
> You can give different containers different sets of privileges, each minimized to the smallest set of permissions it needs to fulfill its function.

Defense in depth
> Containers give another boundary where security protections can be enforced.

Reducing the attack surface

Splitting a monolith into simple microservices can create clean interfaces between them that may, if carefully designed, reduce complexity and hence limit the attack surface. There is a counterargument that adding a complex orchestration layer to coordinate containers introduces another attack surface.

Limiting the blast radius

If a containerized application is compromised, security controls can help constrain the attack within the container and prevent it from affecting the rest of the system.

Segregation of duties

Permissions and credentials can be passed only into the containers that need them, so that the compromise of one set of secrets does not necessarily mean that all secrets are lost.

These benefits sound good, but they are somewhat theoretical. In practice they can easily be outweighed by poor system configuration, bad container image hygiene, or insecure practices. By the end of this book, you should be well armed to avoid the security pitfalls that can appear in a containerized deployment and take advantage of the benefits.

Summary

You've now got a high-level view of the kinds of attacks that can affect a container-based deployment, and an introduction to the security principles that you can apply to defend against those attacks. In the rest of the book you'll delve into the mechanisms that underpin containers so that you can understand how security tools and best-practice processes combine to implement those security principles.

CHAPTER 2

Linux System Calls, Permissions, and Capabilities

In most cases, containers run within a computer running a Linux operating system, and it's going to be helpful to understand some of the fundamental features of Linux so that you can see how they affect security, and in particular how they apply to containers. I'll cover system calls, file-based permissions, and capabilities and conclude with a discussion of privilege escalation. If you're familiar with these concepts, feel free to skip to the next chapter.

This is all important because *containers run Linux processes that are visible from the host*. A containerized process uses system calls and needs permissions and privileges in just the same way that a regular process does. But containers give us some new ways to control how these permissions are assigned at runtime or during the container image build process, which will have a significant impact on security.

System Calls

Applications run in what's called *user space*, which has a lower level of privilege than the operating system kernel. If an application wants to do something like access a file, communicate using a network, or even find the time of day, it has to ask the kernel to do it on the application's behalf. The programmatic interface that the user space code uses to make these requests of the kernel is known as the *system call* or *syscall* interface.

There are some 300+ different system calls, with the number varying according to the version of Linux kernel. Here are a few examples:

read
  read data from a file

write
> write data to a file

open
> open a file for subsequent reading or writing

execve
> run an executable program

chown
> change the owner of a file

clone
> create a new process

Application developers rarely if ever need to worry about system calls directly, as they are usually wrapped in higher-level programming abstractions. The lowest-level abstraction you're likely to come across as an app developer is the glibc library or the Golang syscall package. In practice these are usually wrapped by higher layers of abstractions as well.

 If you would like to learn more about system calls, check out my talk "A Beginner's Guide to Syscalls" (*https://oreil.ly/HrZzJ*), available on O'Reilly's learning platform.

Application code uses system calls in exactly the same way whether it's running in a container or not, but as you will see later in this book, there are security implications to the fact that all the containers on a single host share—that is, they are making system calls to—the same kernel.

Not all applications need all system calls, so—following the principle of least privilege —there are Linux security features that allow users to limit the set of system calls that different programs can access. You'll see how these can be applied to containers in Chapter 8.

I'll return to the subject of user space and kernel-level privileges in Chapter 5. For now let's turn to the question of how Linux controls permissions on files.

File Permissions

On any Linux system, whether you are running containers or not, file permissions are the cornerstone of security. There is a saying that in Linux, everything is a file (*https://oreil.ly/QTxzb*). Application code, data, configuration information, logs, and so on— it's all held in files. Even physical devices like screens and printers are represented as files. Permissions on files determine which users are allowed to access those files and what actions they can perform on the files. These permissions are sometimes referred to as *discretionary access control*, or DAC.

Let's examine this a little more closely.

If you have spent much time in a Linux terminal, you will likely have run the `ls -l` command to retrieve information about files and their attributes.

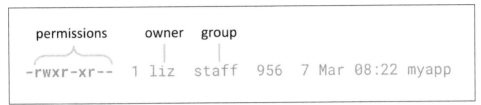

Figure 2-1. Linux file permissions example

In the example in Figure 2-1, you can see a file called *myapp* that is owned by a user called "liz" and is associated with the group "staff." The permission attributes tell you what actions users can perform on this file, depending on their identity. There are nine characters in this output that represent the permissions attributes, and you should think of these in groups of three:

- The first group of three characters describes permissions for the user who owns the file ("liz" in this example).
- The second group gives permissions for members of the file's group (here, "staff").
- The final set shows what any other user (who isn't "liz" or a member of "staff") is permitted to do.

There are three actions that users might be able to perform on this file: read, write, or execute, depending on whether the *r*, *w*, and *x* bits are set. The three characters in each group represent bits that are either on or off, showing which of these three actions are permitted—a dash means that the bit isn't set.

In this example, only the owner of the file can write to it, because the *w* bit is set only in the first group, representing the owner permissions. The owner can execute the file, as can any member of the group "staff." Any user is allowed to read the file, because the *r* bit is set in all three groups.

If you'd like more detail on Linux permissions, there is a good article at *https://oreil.ly/7DKZw*.

There's a good chance that you were already familiar with these *r*, *w*, and *x* bits, but that's not the end of the story. Permissions can be affected by the use of *setuid*, *setgid*, and *sticky* bits. The first two are important from a security perspective because they can allow a process to obtain additional permissions, which an attacker might use for malevolent purposes.

setuid and setgid

Normally, when you execute a file, the process that gets started inherits your user ID. If the file has the *setuid* bit set, the process will have the user ID of the file's owner. The following example uses a copy of the `sleep` executable owned by a non-root user:

```
vagrant@vagrant:~$ ls -l `which sleep`
-rwxr-xr-x 1 root root 35000 Jan 18  2018 /bin/sleep
vagrant@vagrant:~$ cp /bin/sleep ./mysleep
vagrant@vagrant:~$ ls -l mysleep
-rwxr-xr-x 1 vagrant vagrant 35000 Oct 17 08:49 mysleep
```

The `ls` output shows that the copy is owned by the user called `vagrant`. Run this under root by executing `sudo sleep 100`, and in a second terminal you can take a look at the running process—the `100` means you'll have 100 seconds to do this before the process terminates (I have removed some lines from this output for clarity):

```
vagrant@vagrant:~$ ps ajf
 PPID   PID  PGID   SID TTY     TPGID STAT  UID   TIME COMMAND
 1315  1316  1316  1316 pts/0    1502 Ss   1000   0:00 -bash
 1316  1502  1502  1316 pts/0    1502 S+      0   0:00  \_ sudo ./mysleep 100
 1502  1503  1502  1316 pts/0    1502 S+      0   0:00      \_ ./mysleep 100
```

The UID of 0 shows that both the `sudo` process and the `mysleep` process are running under the root UID. Now let's try turning on the *setuid* bit:

```
vagrant@vagrant:~$ chmod +s mysleep
vagrant@vagrant:~$ ls -l mysleep
-rwsr-sr-x 1 vagrant vagrant 35000 Oct 17 08:49 mysleep
```

Run `sudo ./mysleep 100` again, and look at the running processes again from the second terminal:

```
vagrant@vagrant:~$ ps ajf
 PPID   PID  PGID   SID TTY     TPGID STAT  UID   TIME COMMAND
 1315  1316  1316  1316 pts/0    1507 Ss   1000   0:00 -bash
 1316  1507  1507  1316 pts/0    1507 S+      0   0:00  \_ sudo ./mysleep 100
 1507  1508  1507  1316 pts/0    1507 S+   1000   0:00      \_ ./mysleep 100
```

The `sudo` process is still running as root, but this time `mysleep` has taken its user ID from the owner of the file.

This bit is typically used to give a program privileges that it needs but that are not usually extended to regular users. Perhaps the canonical example is the executable ping, which needs permission to open raw network sockets in order to send its ping message. (The mechanism used to give this permission is a capability, which we'll look at in "Linux Capabilities" on page 19.) An administrator might be happy for their users to run ping, but that doesn't mean they are comfortable letting users open raw network sockets for any other purpose they might think of. Instead, the ping executable is often installed with the *setuid* bit set and owned by the root user so that ping can use privileges normally associated with the root user.

I chose my language carefully in that last sentence. As you'll see later in this section, ping actually jumps through a few hoops to avoid running as root. Before I get to that, let's see the *setuid* bit in action.

You can experiment with the permissions required to run ping effectively by taking your own copy as a non-root user. It doesn't really matter whether you are pinging a reachable address; the point is to see whether ping has sufficient permissions to open the raw network socket. Check that you can run ping as expected:

```
vagrant@vagrant:~$ ping 10.0.0.1
PING 10.0.0.1 (10.0.0.1) 56(84) bytes of data.
^C
--- 10.0.0.1 ping statistics ---
2 packets transmitted, 0 received, 100% packet loss, time 1017ms
```

Having established that you can run ping as a non-root user, take a copy and see whether that is also runnable:

```
vagrant@vagrant:~$ ls -l `which ping`
-rwsr-xr-x 1 root root 64424 Jun 28 11:05 /bin/ping
vagrant@vagrant:~$ cp /bin/ping ./myping
vagrant@vagrant:~$ ls -l ./myping
-rwxr-xr-x 1 vagrant vagrant 64424 Nov 24 18:51 ./myping
vagrant@vagrant:~$ ./myping 10.0.0.1
ping: socket: Operation not permitted
```

When you copy an executable, the file ownership attributes are set according to the user ID you're operating as, and the *setuid* bit is not carried over. Running this myping as a regular user doesn't have sufficient privileges to open the raw socket. If you check the permissions bits carefully, you can see that the original ping has the s or *setuid* bit instead of a regular x.

You can try changing the ownership of the file to root (you'll need sudo to be allowed to do this), but still the executable doesn't have sufficient privileges, unless you run as root:

```
vagrant@vagrant:~$ sudo chown root ./myping
vagrant@vagrant:~$ ls -l ./myping
-rwxr-xr-x 1 root vagrant 64424 Nov 24 18:55 ./myping
vagrant@vagrant:~$ ./myping 10.0.0.1
ping: socket: Operation not permitted
```

```
vagrant@vagrant:~$ sudo ./myping 10.0.0.1
PING 10.0.0.1 (10.0.0.1) 56(84) bytes of data.
^C
--- 10.0.0.1 ping statistics ---
2 packets transmitted, 0 received, 100% packet loss, time 1012ms
```

Now set the *setuid* bit on the executable and try again:

```
vagrant@vagrant:~$ sudo chmod +s ./myping
vagrant@vagrant:~$ ls -l ./myping
-rwsr-sr-x 1 root vagrant 64424 Nov 24 18:55 ./myping
vagrant@vagrant:~$ ./myping 10.0.0.1
PING 10.0.0.1 (10.0.0.1) 56(84) bytes of data.
^C
--- 10.0.0.1 ping statistics ---
3 packets transmitted, 0 received, 100% packet loss, time 2052ms
```

As you'll see shortly in "Linux Capabilities" on page 19, there is another way to give myping sufficient privileges to open the socket without the executable having all the privileges associated with root.

Now, this running copy of ping works because it has the *setuid* bit, which allows it to operate as root, but if you use a second terminal to take a look at the process using ps, you might be surprised by the results:

```
vagrant@vagrant:~$ ps uf -C myping
USER      PID %CPU %MEM  VSZ   RSS TTY    STAT START  TIME COMMAND
vagrant  5154  0.0  0.0 18512 2484 pts/1 S+   00:33  0:00 ./myping localhost
```

As you can see, the process is *not* running as root, even though the *setuid* bit is on and the file is owned by root. What's happening here? The answer is that in modern versions of ping, the executable starts off running as root, but it explicitly sets just the capabilities that it needs and then resets its user ID to be that of the original user. This is what I was referring to earlier in this section when I said that it jumps through some hoops.

 If you want to explore this for yourself in more detail, one option is to use strace to see the system calls that the ping (or myping) executable makes. Find the process ID of your shell, and then in a second terminal running as root strace -f -p <shell process ID> will trace out all the system calls from within that shell, including any executables running within it. Look for the setuid() system call, which resets the user ID. You'll see that this happens shortly after some setcap() system calls that set the capabilities that the thread will need.

Not all executables are written to reset the user ID in this way. You can use the copy of sleep from earlier in this chapter to see more normal *setuid* behavior. Change the ownership to root, set the *setuid* bit (this gets reset when you change ownership), and then run it as a non-root user:

```
vagrant@vagrant:~$ sudo chown root mysleep
vagrant@vagrant:~$ sudo chmod +s mysleep
vagrant@vagrant:~$ ls -l ./mysleep
-rwsr-sr-x 1 root vagrant 35000 Dec  2 00:36 ./mysleep
vagrant@vagrant:~$ ./mysleep 100
```

In another terminal you can use `ps` to see that this process is running under root's user ID:

```
vagrant@vagrant:~$ ps uf -C mysleep
USER       PID %CPU %MEM    VSZ   RSS TTY      STAT START   TIME COMMAND
root      6646  0.0  0.0   7468   764 pts/2    S+   00:38   0:00 ./mysleep 100
```

Now that you have experimented with the *setuid* bit, you are in a good position to consider its security implications.

Security implications of setuid

Imagine what would happen if you set *setuid* on, say, `bash`. Any user who runs it would be in a shell, running as the root user. In practice it isn't quite as simple as that, because most shells behave much like `ping` and reset their user ID to avoid being used for such trivial privilege escalations. But it's very easy to write your own program that does *setuid* on itself and then, having already transitioned to root, calls the shell (*https://oreil.ly/viKwm*).

Because *setuid* provides a dangerous pathway to privilege escalation, some container image scanners (covered in Chapter 7) will report on the presence of files with the *setuid* bit set. You can also prevent it from being used with the `--no-new-privileges` flag on a `docker run` command.

The *setuid* bit dates from a time when privileges were much simpler—either your process had root privileges or it didn't. The *setuid* bit provided a mechanism for granting extra privileges to non-root users. Version 2.2 of the Linux kernel introduced more granular control over these extra privileges through *capabilities*.

Linux Capabilities

There are over 30 different capabilities in today's Linux kernel. Capabilities can be assigned to a thread to determine whether that thread can perform certain actions. For example, a thread needs the `CAP_NET_BIND_SERVICE` capability in order to bind to a low-numbered (below 1024) port. `CAP_SYS_BOOT` exists so that arbitrary executables don't have permission to reboot the system. `CAP_SYS_MODULE` is needed to load or unload kernel modules.

I mentioned earlier that the ping tool runs as root just long enough to give itself the required capability that allows a thread to open a raw network socket. This particular capability is called CAP_NET_RAW.

 Consult man capabilities on a Linux machine for detailed information on capabilities.

You can see the capabilities assigned to a process by using the getpcaps command. For example, a process run by a non-root user typically won't have capabilities:

```
vagrant@vagrant:~$ ps
  PID TTY          TIME CMD
22355 pts/0    00:00:00 bash
25058 pts/0    00:00:00 ps
vagrant@vagrant:~$ getpcaps 22355
Capabilities for '22355': =
```

If you run a process as root, it's a different story altogether:

```
vagrant@vagrant:~$ sudo bash
root@vagrant:~# ps
  PID TTY          TIME CMD
25061 pts/0    00:00:00 sudo
25062 pts/0    00:00:00 bash
25070 pts/0    00:00:00 ps
root@vagrant:~# getpcaps 25062
Capabilities for '25062': = cap_chown,cap_dac_override,cap_dac_read_search,
cap_fowner,cap_fsetid,cap_kill,cap_setgid,cap_setuid,cap_setpcap
cap_linux_immutable,cap_net_bind_service,cap_net_broadcast,cap_net_admin,
cap_net_raw,cap_ipc_lock,cap_ipc_owner,cap_sys_module,cap_sys_rawio,
cap_sys_chroot,cap_sys_ptrace,cap_sys_pacct,cap_sys_admin,cap_sys_boot,
cap_sys_nice,cap_sys_resource,cap_sys_time,cap_sys_tty_config,cap_mknod,
cap_lease,cap_audit_write,cap_audit_control,cap_setfcap,cap_mac_override
cap_mac_admin,cap_syslog,cap_wake_alarm,cap_block_suspend,cap_audit_read+ep
```

Files can have capabilities assigned directly to them. Earlier, you saw that a copy of ping wasn't permitted to run under a non-root user without the *setuid* bit. There is another approach: assign the capabilities that it needs directly to the executable file. Take a copy of ping and check that it has normal permissions (no *setuid* bit). This isn't permitted to open the socket:

```
vagrant@vagrant:~$ cp /bin/ping ./myping
vagrant@vagrant:~$ ls -l myping
-rwxr-xr-x 1 vagrant vagrant 64424 Feb 12 18:18 myping
vagrant@vagrant:~$ ./myping 10.0.0.1
ping: socket: Operation not permitted
```

Use setcap to add the CAP_NET_RAW capability to the file, which grants it permission to open raw network sockets. You will need root privileges to change the capabilities. More precisely, you need only the capability CAP_SETFCAP, but this is automatically granted to root:

```
vagrant@vagrant:~$ setcap 'cap_net_raw+p' ./myping
unable to set CAP_SETFCAP effective capability: Operation not permitted
vagrant@vagrant:~$ sudo setcap 'cap_net_raw+p' ./myping
```

This will have no effect on the permissions that ls shows, but you can check the capabilities with getcap:

```
vagrant@vagrant:~$ ls -l myping
-rwxr-xr-x 1 vagrant vagrant 64424 Feb 12 18:18 myping
vagrant@vagrant:~$ getcap ./myping
./myping = cap_net_raw+p
```

This capability allows the copy of ping to operate:

```
vagrant@vagrant:~$ ./myping 10.0.0.1
PING 10.0.0.1 (10.0.0.1) 56(84) bytes of data.
^C
```

> For a more in-depth discussion of the ways that file and process permissions interact, see Adrian Mouat's post on Linux capabilities in practice (*https://oreil.ly/DE8e-*).

Following the principle of least privilege, it's a good idea to grant only the capabilities that are needed for a process to do its job. When you run a container, you get the option to control the capabilities that are permitted, as you'll see in Chapter 8.

Now that you are familiar with the basic concepts of permissions and privileges in Linux, I'd like to turn to the idea of escalating privileges.

Privilege Escalation

The term "privilege escalation" means extending beyond the privileges you were supposed to have so that you can take actions that you shouldn't be permitted to take. To escalate their privileges, an attacker takes advantage of a system vulnerability or poor configuration to grant themselves extra permissions.

Oftentimes, the attacker starts as a non-privileged user and wants to gain root privileges on the machine. A common method of escalating privileges is to look for software that's already running as root and then take advantage of known vulnerabilities in the software. For example, web server software might include a vulnerability that allows an attacker to remotely execute code, such as the Struts vulnerability (*https://*

oreil.ly/ydu-a). If the web server is running as root, anything that is remotely executed by an attacker will run with root privileges. For this reason, it is a good idea to run software as a non-privileged user whenever possible.

As you'll learn later in this book, by default *containers run as root*. This means that compared with a traditional Linux machine, applications running in containers are far more likely to be running as root. An attacker who can take control of a process inside a container still has to somehow escape the container, but once they achieve that, they will be root on the host, and there is no need for any further privilege escalation. Chapter 9 discusses this in more detail.

Even if a container is running as a non-root user, there is potential for privilege escalation based on the Linux permissions mechanisms you have seen earlier in this chapter:

- Container images including with a *setuid* binary
- Additional capabilities granted to a container running as a non-root user

You'll learn about approaches for mitigating these issues later in the book.

Summary

In this chapter you have learned (or revised) some fundamental Linux mechanisms that will be essential to understanding later chapters of this book. They also come into play in security in numerous ways; the container security controls that you will encounter are all built on top of these fundamentals.

Now that you have some basic Linux security controls under your belt, it's time to start looking at the mechanisms that make up containers so that you can understand for yourself how root on the host and in the container are one and the same thing.

CHAPTER 3

Control Groups

In this chapter, you will learn about one of the fundamental building blocks that are used to make containers: *control groups*, more commonly known as *cgroups*.

Cgroups limit the resources, such as memory, CPU, and network input/output, that a group of processes can use. From a security perspective, well-tuned cgroups can ensure that one process can't affect the behavior of other processes by hogging all the resources—for example, using all the CPU or memory to starve other applications. There is also a control group called pid for limiting the total number of processes allowed within a control group, which can prevent the effectiveness of a fork bomb.

 A fork bomb rapidly creates processes that in turn create more processes, leading to an exponential growth in the use of resources that ultimately cripples the machine. This video of a talk I gave a few years back includes a demonstration of using the pid control group to limit the effect of a fork bomb (*https://oreil.ly/Us75y*).

As you will see in detail in Chapter 4, containers run as regular Linux processes, so cgroups can be used to limit the resources available to each container. Let's see how cgroups are organized.

Cgroup Hierarchies

There is a hierarchy of control groups for each type of resource being managed, and each hierarchy is managed by a cgroup controller. Any Linux process is a member of one cgroup of each type, and when it is first created, a process inherits the cgroups of its parent.

The Linux kernel communicates information about cgroups through a set of pseudo-filesystems that typically reside at /sys/fs/cgroup. You can see the different types of cgroups on your system by listing the contents of that directory:

```
root@vagrant:/sys/fs/cgroup$ ls
blkio     cpu,cpuacct  freezer  net_cls          perf_event  systemd
cpu       cpuset       hugetlb  net_cls,net_prio pids        unified
cpuacct   devices      memory   net_prio         rdma
```

Managing cgroups involves reading and writing to the files and directories within these hierarchies. Let's take a look at the memory cgroup as an example:

```
root@vagrant:/sys/fs/cgroup$ ls memory/
cgroup.clone_children              memory.limit_in_bytes
cgroup.event_control               memory.max_usage_in_bytes
cgroup.procs                       memory.move_charge_at_immigrate
cgroup.sane_behavior               memory.numa_stat
init.scope                         memory.oom_control
memory.failcnt                     memory.pressure_level
memory.force_empty                 memory.soft_limit_in_bytes
memory.kmem.failcnt                memory.stat
memory.kmem.limit_in_bytes         memory.swappiness
memory.kmem.max_usage_in_bytes     memory.usage_in_bytes
memory.kmem.slabinfo               memory.use_hierarchy
memory.kmem.tcp.failcnt            notify_on_release
memory.kmem.tcp.limit_in_bytes     release_agent
memory.kmem.tcp.max_usage_in_bytes system.slice
memory.kmem.tcp.usage_in_bytes     tasks
memory.kmem.usage_in_bytes         user.slice
```

You can write to some of these files to manipulate the cgroup, while others contain information written by the kernel to provide data on the state of the cgroup. There's no immediately obvious way to tell which are parameters and which are informational without consulting the documentation (https://oreil.ly/LQxKB), but you can probably guess what some of these files do just from their names. For example, *memory.limit_in_bytes* holds a writable value that sets the amount of memory available to processes in the group; *memory.max_usage_in_bytes* reports the high-water mark of memory usage within the group.

This memory directory is the top level of the hierarchy, and in the absence of other cgroups, this will hold memory information for all running processes. If you want to limit memory usage for a process, you will need to create a new cgroup and then assign the process to it.

Creating Cgroups

Creating a subdirectory inside this memory directory creates a cgroup, and the kernel automatically populates the directory with the various files that represent parameters and statistics about the cgroup:

```
root@vagrant:/sys/fs/cgroup$ mkdir memory/liz
root@vagrant:/sys/fs/cgroup$ ls memory/liz/
cgroup.clone_children                 memory.limit_in_bytes
cgroup.event_control                  memory.max_usage_in_bytes
cgroup.procs                          memory.move_charge_at_immigrate
memory.failcnt                        memory.numa_stat
memory.force_empty                    memory.oom_control
memory.kmem.failcnt                   memory.pressure_level
memory.kmem.limit_in_bytes            memory.soft_limit_in_bytes
memory.kmem.max_usage_in_bytes        memory.stat
memory.kmem.slabinfo                  memory.swappiness
memory.kmem.tcp.failcnt               memory.usage_in_bytes
memory.kmem.tcp.limit_in_bytes        memory.use_hierarchy
memory.kmem.tcp.max_usage_in_bytes    notify_on_release
memory.kmem.tcp.usage_in_bytes        tasks
memory.kmem.usage_in_bytes
```

The details of what each of these different files means are beyond the scope of this book, but some of the files hold parameters that you can manipulate to define limits for the control group, and others communicate statistics about the current use of resources in the control group. You could probably make an educated guess that, for example, *memory.usage_in_bytes* is the file that describes how much memory is currently being used by the control group. The maximum that the cgroup is allowed to use is defined by *memory.limit_in_bytes*.

When you start a container, the runtime creates new cgroups for it. You can use a utility called lscgroup (on Ubuntu this is installed via the cgroup-tools package) to help see these cgroups from the host. Since there are quite a lot of them, let's just look at the difference in memory cgroups before and after starting a new container with runc. In one terminal window, take a snapshot of the memory cgroups:

```
root@vagrant:~$ lscgroup memory:/ > before.memory
```

Start a container in a second terminal:

```
vagrant@vagrant:alpine-bundle$ sudo runc run sh
/ $
```

Then take another snapshot and compare the two:

```
root@vagrant:~$ lscgroup memory:/ > after.memory
root@vagrant:~$ diff before.memory after.memory
4a5
> memory:/user.slice/user-1000.slice/session-43.scope/sh
```

The hierarchy is relative to the root of the memory cgroup, which is conventionally located at */sys/fs/cgroup/memory*. While the container is still running, we can inspect the cgroup from the host:

```
root@vagrant:/sys/fs/cgroup/memory$ ls user.slice/user-1000.slice/session-43.sco
pe/sh/
cgroup.clone_children                 memory.limit_in_bytes
```

```
cgroup.event_control                    memory.max_usage_in_bytes
cgroup.procs                            memory.move_charge_at_immigrate
memory.failcnt                          memory.numa_stat
memory.force_empty                      memory.oom_control
memory.kmem.failcnt                     memory.pressure_level
memory.kmem.limit_in_bytes              memory.soft_limit_in_bytes
memory.kmem.max_usage_in_bytes          memory.stat
memory.kmem.slabinfo                    memory.swappiness
memory.kmem.tcp.failcnt                 memory.usage_in_bytes
memory.kmem.tcp.limit_in_bytes          memory.use_hierarchy
memory.kmem.tcp.max_usage_in_bytes      notify_on_release
memory.kmem.tcp.usage_in_bytes          tasks
memory.kmem.usage_in_bytes
```

From inside the container, the list of its own cgroups is available from the /proc directory:

```
/ $ cat /proc/$$/cgroup
12:cpu,cpuacct:/sh
11:cpuset:/sh
10:hugetlb:/sh
9:blkio:/sh
8:memory:/user.slice/user-1000.slice/session-43.scope/sh
7:pids:/user.slice/user-1000.slice/session-43.scope/sh
6:freezer:/sh
5:devices:/user.slice/sh
4:net_cls,net_prio:/sh
3:rdma:/
2:perf_event:/sh
1:name=systemd:/user.slice/user-1000.slice/session-43.scope/sh
0::/user.slice/user-1000.slice/session-43.scope
```

Notice that the memory cgroup is exactly what you found from the host's perspective. Once you have a cgroup, you can modify parameters within it by writing to the appropriate files.

You might be wondering about the user.slice/user-1000 parts of the preceding cgroup listing. This relates to systemd, which automatically creates some cgroup hierarchies for its own approach to resource control. Red Hat provides a readable description (*https://oreil.ly/i4OWd*) of this if you are interested in learning more.

Setting Resource Limits

You can see how much memory is available to the cgroup by examining the contents of its *memory.limit_in_bytes* file:

```
root@vagrant:/sys/fs/cgroup/memory$ cat user.slice/user-1000.slice/session-43.sco
pe/sh/memory.limit_in_bytes
9223372036854771712
```

By default the memory isn't limited, so this giant number represents all the memory available to the virtual machine I'm using to generate this example.

If a process is allowed to consume unlimited memory, it can starve other processes on the same host. This might happen inadvertently through a memory leak in an application, or it could be the result of a resource exhaustion attack (*https://oreil.ly/npkSE*) that takes advantage of a memory leak to deliberately use as much memory as possible. By setting limits on the memory and other resources that one process can access, you can reduce the effects of this kind of attack and ensure that other processes can carry on as normal.

You can modify the *config.json* file in `runc`'s runtime bundle to restrict memory that it will assign to the cgroup when it creates a container. Cgroup limits are configured in the `linux:resources` section of *config.json*, like this:

```
"linux": {
        "resources": {
                "memory": {
                        "limit": 1000000
                },
                ...
        }
}
```

You will need to stop the container and rerun the `runc` command for this new configuration to be picked up. If you use the same name for the container, the cgroup name will be the same (but you can check by running `cat /proc/$$/cgroup` inside the container). Now you'll find that the `memory.limit_in_bytes` parameter is approximately what you configured as the limit—presumably, to the nearest kB:

```
root@vagrant:/sys/fs/cgroup/memory$ cat user.slice/user-1000.slice/session-43.sco
pe/sh/memory.limit_in_bytes
999424
```

It's `runc` that changed this value. To set a limit for a cgroup, you simply have to write the value into the file that corresponds to the parameter you want to limit.

This shows how the limits are set, but the final piece of the cgroups puzzle is to see how processes get assigned into cgroups.

Assigning a Process to a Cgroup

Much like setting resource limits, assigning a process to a cgroup is a simple matter of writing its process ID into the `cgroup.procs` file for the cgroup. In the following example, 29903 is the process ID of a shell:

```
root@vagrant:/sys/fs/cgroup/memory/liz$ echo 100000 > memory.limit_in_bytes
root@vagrant:/sys/fs/cgroup/memory/liz$ cat memory.limit_in_bytes
98304
```

```
root@vagrant:/sys/fs/cgroup/memory/liz$ echo 29903 > cgroup.procs
root@vagrant:/sys/fs/cgroup/memory/liz$ cat cgroup.procs
29903
root@vagrant:/sys/fs/cgroup/memory/liz$ cat /proc/29903/cgroup | grep memory
8:memory:/liz
```

The shell is now a member of the cgroup, with its memory limited to a little under 100kB. This isn't a lot to play with, so even trying to run ls from inside the shell breaches the cgroup limit:

```
$ ls
Killed
```

The process gets killed when it attempts to exceed the memory limit.

Docker Using Cgroups

You've seen how cgroups are manipulated by modifying the files in the cgroup filesystem for a particular type of resource. It's straightforward to see this in action in Docker.

 To follow along with these examples, you will need Docker running directly on a Linux (virtual) machine. If you're running Docker for Mac/Windows, it's running within a virtual machine, which means (as you'll see in Chapter 5) that these examples won't work for you, because the Docker daemon and containers are running using a separate kernel within that virtual machine.

Docker automatically creates its own cgroups of each type. You can see them by looking for directories called docker within the cgroups hierarchy:

```
root@vagrant:/sys/fs/cgroup$ ls */docker | grep docker
blkio/docker:
cpuacct/docker:
cpu,cpuacct/docker:
cpu/docker:
cpuset/docker:
devices/docker:
freezer/docker:
hugetlb/docker:
memory/docker:
net_cls/docker:
net_cls,net_prio/docker:
net_prio/docker:
perf_event/docker:
pids/docker:
systemd/docker:
```

When you start a container, it automatically creates another set of cgroups within the docker cgroups. Create a container and give it a memory limit that we can observe within the memory cgroup. This example runs a container in the background that sleeps long enough for you to see its cgroups:

```
root@vagrant:~$ docker run --rm --memory 100M -d alpine sleep 10000
68fb008c5fd3f9067e1aa245b4522a9f3675720d8953371ecfcf2e9faf91b8a0
```

If you look in the cgroups hierarchy, you will see new cgroups created for this container, using the container ID as a cgroup name:

```
root@vagrant:/sys/fs/cgroup$ ls memory/docker/
68fb008c5fd3f9067e1aa245b4522a9f3675720d8953371ecfcf2e9faf91b8a0
cgroup.clone_children
cgroup.event_control
cgroup.procs
memory.failcnt
memory.force_empty
memory.kmem.failcnt
memory.kmem.limit_in_bytes
memory.kmem.max_usage_in_bytes
...
```

Check the limit in bytes within this memory cgroup:

```
root@vagrant:/sys/fs/cgroup$ cat memory/docker/68fb008c5fd3f9067e1aa245b4522a9f36
75720d8953371ecfcf2e9faf91b8a0/memory.limit_in_bytes
104857600
```

You can also confirm that the sleeping process is a member of the cgroup:

```
root@vagrant:/sys/fs/cgroup$ cat memory/docker/68fb008c5fd3f9067e1aa245b4522a9f36
75720d8953371ecfcf2e9faf91b8a0/cgroup.procs
19824
root@vagrant:/sys/fs/cgroup$ ps -eaf | grep sleep
root     19824 19789  0 18:22 ?        00:00:00 sleep 10000
root     20486 18862  0 18:28 pts/1    00:00:00 grep --color=auto sleep
```

Cgroups V2

There has been a version 2 of cgroups available in the Linux kernel since 2016, and Fedora became the first Linux distro to default to cgroups v2 in mid-2019. However, at the time of writing, the most popular container runtime implementations assume version 1 of cgroups and don't support v2 (though there is ongoing work, which Akihiro Suda summarized nicely in a blog post (*https://oreil.ly/pDTZ6*)).

The biggest difference is that in cgroups v2 a process can't join different groups for different controllers. In v1 a process could join /sys/fs/cgroup/memory/mygroup and /sys/fs/cgroup/pids/yourgroup. In v2 things are simpler: the process joins /sys/fs/cgroup/ourgroup and is subject to all the controllers for ourgroup.

Cgroups v2 also has better support for rootless containers so that resource limits can be applied to them. You'll come to this in "Rootless Containers" on page 109.

Summary

Cgroups limit the resources available to different Linux processes. You don't have to be using containers to take advantage of cgroups, but Docker and other container runtimes provide a convenient interface for using them: it's very easy to set resource limits at the point where you run a container, and those limits are policed by cgroups.

Constraining resources provides protection against a class of attacks that attempt to disrupt your deployment by consuming excessive resources, thereby starving legitimate applications. It's recommended that you set memory and CPU limits when you run your container applications.

Now that you know how resources are constrained in containers, you are ready to learn about the other pieces of the puzzle that make up containers: namespaces and changing the root directory. Move on to Chapter 4 to find out how these work.

CHAPTER 4

Container Isolation

This is the chapter in which you'll find out how containers really work! This will be essential to understanding the extent to which containers are isolated from each other and from the host. You will be able to assess for yourself the strength of the security boundary that surrounds a container.

As you'll know if you have ever run `docker exec <image> bash`, a container looks a lot like a virtual machine from the inside. If you have shell access to a container and run `ps`, you can see only the processes that are running inside it. The container has its own network stack, and it seems to have its own filesystem with a root directory that bears no relation to root on the host. You can run containers with limited resources, such as a restricted amount of memory or a fraction of the available CPUs. This all happens using the Linux features that we're going to delve into in this chapter.

However much they might superficially resemble each other, it's important to realize that containers *aren't* virtual machines, and in Chapter 5 we'll take a look at the differences between these two types of isolation. In my experience, really understanding and being able to contrast the two is absolutely key to grasping the extent to which traditional security measures can be effective in containers, and to identifying where container-specific tooling is necessary.

You'll see how containers are built out of Linux constructs such as namespaces and `chroot`, along with cgroups, which were covered in Chapter 3. With an understanding of these constructs under your belt, you'll have a feeling for how well protected your applications are when they run inside containers.

Although the general concepts of these constructs are fairly straightforward, the way they work together with other features of the Linux kernel can be complex. Container escape vulnerabilities (for example, CVE-2019-5736 (*https://oreil.ly/NtcRv*), a serious vulnerability discovered in both `runc` and LXC) have been based on subtleties in the way that namespaces, capabilities, and filesystems interact.

Linux Namespaces

If cgroups control the resources that a process can use, *namespaces* control what it can see. By putting a process in a namespace, you can restrict the resources that are visible to that process.

The origins of namespaces date back to the Plan 9 (*https://oreil.ly/BCi9W*) operating system. At the time, most operating systems had a single "name space" of files. Unix systems allowed the mounting of filesystems, but they would all be mounted into the same system-wide view of all filenames. In Plan 9, each process was part of a process group that had its own "name space" abstraction, the hierarchy of files (and file-like objects) that this group of processes could see. Each process group could mount its own set of filesystems without seeing each other.

The first namespace was introduced to the Linux kernel in version 2.4.19 back in 2002. This was the mount namespace, and it followed similar functionality to that in Plan 9. Nowadays there are several different kinds of namespace supported by Linux:

- Unix Timesharing System (UTS)—this sounds complicated, but to all intents and purposes this namespace is really just about the hostname and domain names for the system that a process is aware of.
- Process IDs
- Mount points
- Network
- User and group IDs
- Inter-process communications (IPC)
- Control groups (cgroups)

It's possible that more resources will be namespaced in future revisions of the Linux kernel. For example, there have been discussions (*https://oreil.ly/NZqb-*) about having a namespace for time.

A process is always in exactly one namespace of each type. When you start a Linux system it has a single namespace of each type, but as you'll see, you can create additional namespaces and assign processes into them. You can easily see the namespaces on your machine using the `lsns` command:

```
vagrant@myhost:~$ lsns
        NS TYPE    NPROCS   PID USER    COMMAND
4026531835 cgroup       3 28459 vagrant /lib/systemd/systemd --user
4026531836 pid          3 28459 vagrant /lib/systemd/systemd --user
```

```
4026531837 user        3 28459 vagrant /lib/systemd/systemd --user
4026531838 uts         3 28459 vagrant /lib/systemd/systemd --user
4026531839 ipc         3 28459 vagrant /lib/systemd/systemd --user
4026531840 mnt         3 28459 vagrant /lib/systemd/systemd --user
4026531992 net         3 28459 vagrant /lib/systemd/systemd --user
```

This looks nice and neat, and there is one namespace for each of the types I mentioned previously. Sadly, this is an incomplete picture! The man page (*https://oreil.ly/ nd0Eh*) for lsns tells us that it "reads information directly from the */proc* filesystem and for non-root users it may return incomplete information." Let's see what you get when you run as root:

```
vagrant@myhost:~$ sudo lsns
        NS TYPE    NPROCS   PID USER           COMMAND
4026531835 cgroup      93     1 root           /sbin/init
4026531836 pid         93     1 root           /sbin/init
4026531837 user        93     1 root           /sbin/init
4026531838 uts         93     1 root           /sbin/init
4026531839 ipc         93     1 root           /sbin/init
4026531840 mnt         89     1 root           /sbin/init
4026531860 mnt          1    15 root           kdevtmpfs
4026531992 net         93     1 root           /sbin/init
4026532170 mnt          1 14040 root           /lib/systemd/systemd-udevd
4026532171 mnt          1   451 systemd-network /lib/systemd/systemd-networkd
4026532190 mnt          1   617 systemd-resolve /lib/systemd/systemd-resolved
```

The root user can see some additional mount namespaces, and there are a lot more processes visible to root than were visible to the non-root user. The reason to show you this is to note that when we are using lsns, we should run as root (or use sudo) to get the complete picture.

Let's explore how you can use namespaces to create something that behaves like what we call a "container."

 The examples in this chapter use Linux shell commands to create a container. If you would like to try creating a container using the Go programming language, you will find instructions at *https:// github.com/lizrice/containers-from-scratch*.

Isolating the Hostname

Let's start with the namespace for the Unix Timesharing System (UTS). As mentioned previously, this covers the hostname and domain names. By putting a process in its own UTS namespace, you can change the hostname for this process independently of the hostname of the machine or virtual machine on which it's running.

If you open a terminal on Linux, you can see the hostname:

```
vagrant@myhost:~$ hostname
myhost
```

Most (perhaps all?) container systems give each container a random ID. By default this ID is used as the hostname. You can see this by running a container and getting shell access. For example, in Docker you could do the following:

```
vagrant@myhost:~$ docker run --rm -it --name hello ubuntu bash
root@cdf75e7a6c50:/$ hostname
cdf75e7a6c50
```

Incidentally, you can see in this example that even if you give the container a name in Docker (here I specified --name hello), that name isn't used for the hostname of the container.

The container can have its own hostname because Docker created it with its own UTS namespace. You can explore the same thing by using the unshare command to create a process that has a UTS namespace of its own.

As it's described on the man page (seen by running man unshare), unshare lets you "run a program with some namespaces unshared from the parent." Let's dig a little deeper into that description. When you "run a program," the kernel creates a new process and executes the program in it. This is done from the context of a running process—the *parent*—and the new process will be referred to as the *child*. The word "unshare" means that, rather than sharing namespaces of its parent, the child is going to be given its own.

Let's give it a try. You need to have root privileges to do this, hence the sudo at the start of the line:

```
vagrant@myhost:~$ sudo unshare --uts sh
$ hostname
myhost
$ hostname experiment
$ hostname
experiment
$ exit
vagrant@myhost:~$ hostname
myhost
```

This runs a sh shell in a new process that has a new UTS namespace. Any programs you run inside the shell will inherit its namespaces. When you run the hostname command, it executes in the new UTS namespace that has been isolated from that of the host machine.

If you were to open another terminal window to the same host before the exit, you could confirm that the hostname hasn't changed for the whole (virtual) machine. You can change the hostname on the host without affecting the hostname that the namespaced process is aware of, and vice versa.

This is a key component of the way containers work. Namespaces give them a set of resources (in this case the hostname) that are independent of the host machine, and of other containers. But we are still talking about a process that is being run by the same Linux kernel. This has security implications that I'll discuss later in the chapter. For now, let's look at another example of a namespace by seeing how you can give a container its own view of running processes.

Isolating Process IDs

If you run the ps command inside a Docker container, you can see only the processes running inside that container and none of the processes running on the host:

```
vagrant@myhost:~$ docker run --rm -it --name hello ubuntu bash
root@cdf75e7a6c50:/$ ps -eaf
UID          PID  PPID  C STIME TTY          TIME CMD
root           1     0  0 18:41 pts/0    00:00:00 bash
root          10     1  0 18:42 pts/0    00:00:00 ps -eaf
root@cdf75e7a6c50:/$ exit
vagrant@myhost:~$
```

This is achieved with the process ID namespace, which restricts the set of process IDs that are visible. Try running unshare again, but this time specifying that you want a new PID namespace with the --pid flag:

```
vagrant@myhost:~$ sudo unshare --pid sh
$ whoami
root
$ whoami
sh: 2: Cannot fork
$ whoami
sh: 3: Cannot fork
$ ls
sh: 4: Cannot fork
$ exit
vagrant@myhost:~$
```

This doesn't seem very successful—it's not possible to run any commands after the first whoami! But there are some interesting artifacts in this output.

The first process under sh seems to have worked OK, but every command after that fails due to an inability to fork. The error is output in the form <command>: <process ID>: <message>, and you can see that the process IDs are incrementing each time. Given the sequence, it would be reasonable to assume that the first whoami ran as process ID 1. That is a clue that the PID namespace is working in some fashion, in that the process ID numbering has restarted. But it's pretty much useless if you can't run more than one process!

There are clues to what the problem is in the description of the --fork flag in the man page for unshare: "Fork the specified program as a child process of unshare rather than running it directly. This is useful when creating a new pid namespace."

You can explore this by running ps to view the process hierarchy from a second terminal window:

```
vagrant@myhost:~$ ps fa
  PID TTY        STAT    TIME COMMAND
...
30345 pts/0      Ss     0:00 -bash
30475 pts/0      S      0:00  \_ sudo unshare --pid sh
30476 pts/0      S      0:00      \_ sh
```

The sh process is not a child of unshare; it's a child of the sudo process.

Now try the same thing with the --fork parameter:

```
vagrant@myhost:~$ sudo unshare --pid --fork sh
$ whoami
root
$ whoami
root
```

This is progress, in that you can now run more than one command before running into the "Cannot fork" error. If you look at the process hierarchy again from a second terminal, you'll see an important difference:

```
vagrant@myhost:~$ ps fa
  PID TTY        STAT    TIME COMMAND
...
30345 pts/0      Ss     0:00 -bash
30470 pts/0      S      0:00  \_ sudo unshare --pid --fork sh
30471 pts/0      S      0:00      \_ unshare --pid --fork sh
30472 pts/0      S      0:00          \_ sh
...
```

With the --fork parameter, the sh shell is running as a child of the unshare process, and you can successfully run as many different child commands as you choose within this shell.

Given that the shell is within its own process ID namespace, the results of running ps inside it might be surprising:

```
vagrant@myhost:~$ sudo unshare --pid --fork sh
$ ps
  PID TTY          TIME CMD
14511 pts/0     00:00:00 sudo
14512 pts/0     00:00:00 unshare
14513 pts/0     00:00:00 sh
14515 pts/0     00:00:00 ps
$ ps -eaf
UID          PID  PPID  C STIME TTY          TIME CMD
```

```
root            1      0    0  Mar27  ?        00:00:02  /sbin/init
root            2      0    0  Mar27  ?        00:00:00  [kthreadd]
root            3      2    0  Mar27  ?        00:00:00  [ksoftirqd/0]
root            5      2    0  Mar27  ?        00:00:00  [kworker/0:0H]
...many more lines of output about processes...
$ exit
vagrant@myhost:~$
```

As you can see, ps is still showing all the processes on the whole host, despite running inside a new process ID namespace. If you want the ps behavior that you would see in a Docker container, it's not sufficient just to use a new process ID namespace, and the reason for this is included in the man page for ps: "This ps works by reading the virtual files in /proc."

Let's take a look at the /proc directory to see what virtual files this is referring to. Your system will look similar, but not exactly the same, as it will be running a different set of processes:

```
vagrant@myhost:~$ ls /proc
1      14553  292    467    cmdline    modules
10     14585  3      5      consoles   mounts
1009   14586  30087  53     cpuinfo    mpt
1010   14664  30108  538    crypto     mtrr
1015   14725  30120  54     devices    net
1016   14749  30221  55     diskstats  pagetypeinfo
1017   15     30224  56     dma        partitions
1030   156    30256  57     driver     sched_debug
1034   157    30257  58     execdomains schedstat
1037   158    30283  59     fb         scsi
1044   159    313    60     filesystems self
1053   16     314    61     fs         slabinfo
1063   160    315    62     interrupts softirqs
1076   161    34     63     iomem      stat
1082   17     35     64     ioports    swaps
11     18     3509   65     irq        sys
1104   19     3512   66     kallsyms   sysrq-trigger
1111   2      36     7      kcore      sysvipc
1175   20     37     72     keys       thread-self
1194   21     378    8      key-users  timer_list
12     22     385    85     kmsg       timer_stats
1207   23     392    86     kpagecgroup tty
1211   24     399    894    kpagecount uptime
1215   25     401    9      kpageflags version
12426  26     403    966    loadavg    version_signature
125    263    407    acpi   locks      vmallocinfo
13     27     409    buddyinfo mdstat  vmstat
14046  28     412    bus    meminfo    zoneinfo
14087  29     427    cgroups misc
```

Every numbered directory in /proc corresponds to a process ID, and there is a lot of interesting information about a process inside its directory. For example, /proc/

`<pid>/exe` is a symbolic link to the executable that's being run inside this particular process, as you can see in the following example:

```
vagrant@myhost:~$ ps
  PID TTY          TIME CMD
28441 pts/1    00:00:00 bash
28558 pts/1    00:00:00 ps
vagrant@myhost:~$ ls /proc/28441
attr             fdinfo       numa_maps        smaps
autogroup        gid_map      oom_adj          smaps_rollup
auxv             io           oom_score        stack
cgroup           limits       oom_score_adj    stat
clear_refs       loginuid     pagemap          statm
cmdline          map_files    patch_state      status
comm             maps         personality      syscall
coredump_filter  mem          projid_map       task
cpuset           mountinfo    root             timers
cwd              mounts       sched            timerslack_ns
environ          mountstats   schedstat        uid_map
exe              net          sessionid        wchan
fd               ns           setgroups
vagrant@myhost:~$ ls -l /proc/28441/exe
lrwxrwxrwx 1 vagrant vagrant 0 Oct 10 13:32 /proc/28441/exe -> /bin/bash
```

Irrespective of the process ID namespace it's running in, ps is going to look in `/proc` for information about running processes. In order to have ps return only the information about the processes inside the new namespace, there needs to be a separate copy of the `/proc` directory, where the kernel can write information about the name-spaced processes. Given that `/proc` is a directory directly under root, this means changing the root directory.

Changing the Root Directory

From within a container, you don't see the host's entire filesystem; instead, you see a subset, because the root directory gets changed as the container is created.

You can change the root directory in Linux with the `chroot` command. This effectively moves the root directory for the current process to point to some other location within the filesystem. Once you have done a `chroot` command, you lose access to anything that was higher in the file hierarchy than your current root directory, since there is no way to go any higher than root within the filesystem, as illustrated in Figure 4-1.

The description in `chroot`'s man page reads as follows: "Run COMMAND with root directory set to NEWROOT. [...] If no command is given, run *${SHELL} -i* (default: */bin/sh -i*)."

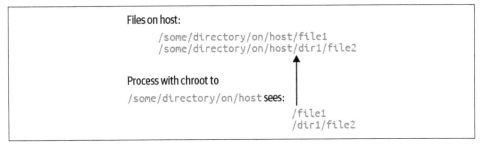

Figure 4-1. Changing root so a process only sees a subset of the filesystem

From this you can see that chroot doesn't just change the directory, but also runs a command, falling back to running a shell if you don't specify a different command.

Create a new directory and try to chroot into it:

```
vagrant@myhost:~$ mkdir new_root
vagrant@myhost:~$ sudo chroot new_root
chroot: failed to run command '/bin/bash': No such file or directory
vagrant@myhost:~$ sudo chroot new_root ls
chroot: failed to run command 'ls': No such file or directory
```

This doesn't work! The problem is that once you are inside the new root directory, there is no bin directory inside this root, so it's impossible to run the /bin/bash shell. Similarly, if you try to run the ls command, it's not there. You'll need the files for any commands you want to run to be available within the new root. This is exactly what happens in a "real" container: the container is instantiated from a container image, which encapsulates the filesystem that the container sees. If an executable isn't present within that filesystem, the container won't be able to find and run it.

Why not try running Alpine Linux within your container? Alpine is a fairly minimal Linux distribution designed for containers. You'll need to start by downloading the filesystem:

```
vagrant@myhost:~$ mkdir alpine
vagrant@myhost:~$ cd alpine
vagrant@myhost:~/alpine$ curl -o alpine.tar.gz http://dl-cdn.alpinelinux.org/
alpine/v3.10/releases/x86_64/alpine-minirootfs-3.10.0-x86_64.tar.gz
  % Total    % Received % Xferd  Average Speed   Time    Time     Time  Current
                                 Dload  Upload   Total   Spent    Left  Speed
100 2647k  100 2647k    0     0  16.6M      0 --:--:-- --:--:-- --:--:-- 16.6M
vagrant@myhost:~/alpine$ tar xvf alpine.tar.gz
```

At this point you have a copy of the Alpine filesystem inside the alpine directory you created. Remove the compressed version and move back to the parent directory:

```
vagrant@myhost:~/alpine$ rm alpine.tar.gz
vagrant@myhost:~/alpine$ cd ..
```

You can explore the contents of the filesystem with `ls alpine` to see that it looks like the root of a Linux filesystem with directories such as `bin`, `lib`, `var`, `tmp`, and so on.

Now that you have the Alpine distribution unpacked, you can use `chroot` to move into the `alpine` directory, provided you supply a command that exists within that directory's hierarchy.

It's slightly more subtle than that, because the executable has to be in the new process's path. This process inherits the parent's environment, including the `PATH` environment variable. The `bin` directory within `alpine` has become `/bin` for the new process, and assuming that your regular path includes `/bin`, you can pick up the `ls` executable from that directory without specifying its path explicitly:

```
vagrant@myhost:~$ sudo chroot alpine ls
bin     etc     lib     mnt     proc    run     srv     tmp     var
dev     home    media   opt     root    sbin    sys     usr
vagrant@myhost:~$
```

Notice that it is only the child process (in this example, the process that ran `ls`) that gets the new root directory. When that process finishes, control returns to the parent process. If you run a shell as the child process, it won't complete immediately, so that makes it easier to see the effects of changing the root directory:

```
vagrant@myhost:~$ sudo chroot alpine sh
/ $ ls
bin     etc     lib     mnt     proc    run     srv     tmp     var
dev     home    media   opt     root    sbin    sys     usr
/ $ whoami
root
/ $ exit
vagrant@myhost:~$
```

If you try to run the bash shell, it won't work. This is because the Alpine distribution doesn't include it, so it's not present inside the new root directory. If you tried the same thing with the filesystem of a distribution like Ubuntu, which does include bash, it would work.

To summarize, `chroot` literally "changes the root" for a process. After changing the root, the process (and its children) will be able to access only the files and directories that are lower in the hierarchy than the new root directory.

In addition to chroot, there is a system call called pivot_root. For the purposes of this chapter, whether chroot or pivot_root is used is an implementation detail; the key point is that a container needs to have its own root directory. I have used chroot in these examples because it is slightly simpler and more familiar to many people.

There are security advantages to using pivot_root over chroot, so in practice you should find the former if you look at the source code of a container runtime implementation. The main difference is that pivot_root takes advantage of the mount namespace; the old root is no longer mounted and is therefore no longer accessible within that mount namespace. The chroot system call doesn't take this approach, leaving the old root accessible via mount points.

You have now seen how a container can be given its own root filesystem. I'll discuss this further in Chapter 6, but right now let's see how having its own root filesystem allows the kernel to show a container just a restricted view of namespaced resources.

Combine Namespacing and Changing the Root

So far you have seen namespacing and changing the root as two separate things, but you can combine the two by running chroot in a new namespace:

```
me@myhost:~$ sudo unshare --pid --fork chroot alpine sh
/ $ ls
bin    etc   lib    mnt   proc   run   srv   tmp   var
dev    home  media  opt   root   sbin  sys   usr
```

If you recall from earlier in this chapter (see "Isolating Process IDs" on page 35), giving the container its own root directory allows it to create a /proc directory for the container that's independent of /proc on the host. For this to be populated with process information, you will need to mount it as a pseudofilesystem of type proc. With the combination of a process ID namespace and an independent /proc directory, ps will now show just the processes that are inside the process ID namespace:

```
/ $ mount -t proc proc proc
/ $ ps
PID   USER     TIME  COMMAND
    1 root     0:00 sh
    6 root     0:00 ps
/ $ exit
vagrant@myhost:~$
```

Success! It has been more complex than isolating the container's hostname, but through the combination of creating a process ID namespace, changing the root directory, and mounting a pseudofilesystem to handle process information, you can limit a container so that it has a view only of its own processes.

There are more namespaces left to explore. Let's see the mount namespace next.

Mount Namespace

Typically you don't want a container to have all the same filesystem mounts as its host. Giving the container its own mount namespace achieves this separation.

Here's an example that creates a simple bind mount for a process with its own mount namespace:

```
vagrant@myhost:~$ sudo unshare --mount sh
$ mkdir source
$ touch source/HELLO
$ ls source
HELLO
$ mkdir target
$ ls target
$ mount --bind source target
$ ls target
HELLO
```

Once the bind mount is in place, the contents of the source directory are also available in target. If you look at all the mounts from within this process, there will probably be a lot of them, but the following command finds the target you created if you followed the preceding example:

```
$ findmnt target
TARGET      SOURCE              FSTYPE OPTIONS
/home/vagrant/target
            /dev/mapper/vagrant--vg-root[/home/vagrant/source]
                                ext4   rw,relatime,errors=remount-ro,data=ordered
```

From the host's perspective, this isn't visible, which you can prove by running the same command from another terminal window and confirming that it doesn't return anything.

Try running findmnt from within the mount namespace again, but this time without any parameters, and you will get a long list. You might be thinking that it seems wrong for a container to be able to see all the mounts on the host. This is a very similar situation to what you saw with the process ID namespace: the kernel uses the /proc/<PID>/mounts directory to communicate information about mount points for each process. If you create a process with its own mount namespace but it is using the host's /proc directory, you'll find that its */proc/<PID>/mounts* file includes all the preexisting host mounts. (You can simply cat this file to get a list of mounts.)

To get a fully isolated set of mounts for the containerized process, you will need to combine creating a new mount namespace with a new root filesystem and a new proc mount, like this:

```
vagrant@myhost:~$ sudo unshare --mount chroot alpine sh
/ $ mount -t proc proc proc
/ $ mount
proc on /proc type proc (rw,relatime)
/ $ mkdir source
/ $ touch source/HELLO
/ $ mkdir target
/ $ mount --bind source target
/ $ mount
proc on /proc type proc (rw,relatime)
/dev/sda1 on /target type ext4 (rw,relatime,data=ordered)
```

Alpine Linux doesn't come with the findmnt command, so this example uses mount with no parameters to generate the list of mounts. (If you are cynical about this change, try the earlier example with mount instead of findmnt to check that you get the same results.)

You may be familiar with the concept of mounting host directories into a container using docker run -v <host directory>:<container directory> .... To achieve this, after the root filesystem has been put in place for the container, the target container directory is created and then the source host directory gets bind mounted into that target. Because each container has its own mount namespace, host directories mounted like this are not visible from other containers.

> If you create a mount that is visible to the host, it won't automatically get cleaned up when your "container" process terminates. You will need to destroy it using umount. This also applies to the /proc pseudofilesystems. They won't do any particular harm, but if you like to keep things tidy, you can remove them with umount proc. The system won't let you unmount the final /proc used by the host.

Network Namespace

The network namespace allows a container to have its own view of network interfaces and routing tables. When you create a process with its own network namespace, you can see it with lsns:

```
vagrant@myhost:~$ sudo lsns -t net
        NS TYPE NPROCS PID USER     NETNSID NSFS COMMAND
4026531992 net       93   1 root unassigned      /sbin/init
vagrant@myhost:~$ sudo unshare --net bash
root@myhost:~$ lsns -t net
        NS TYPE NPROCS  PID USER     NETNSID NSFS COMMAND
4026531992 net       92    1 root unassigned      /sbin/init
4026532192 net        2 28586 root unassigned      bash
```

You might come across the `ip netns` command, but that is not much use to us here. Using `unshare --net` creates an anonymous network namespace, and anonymous namespaces don't appear in the output from `ip netns list`.

When you put a process into its own network namespace, it starts with just the loopback interface:

```
vagrant@myhost:~$ sudo unshare --net bash
root@myhost:~$ ip a
1: lo: <LOOPBACK> mtu 65536 qdisc noop state DOWN group default qlen 1000
    link/loopback 00:00:00:00:00:00 brd 00:00:00:00:00:00
```

With nothing but a loopback interface, your container won't be able to communicate. To give it a path to the outside world, you create a virtual Ethernet interface—or more strictly, a pair of virtual Ethernet interfaces. These act as if they were the two ends of a metaphorical cable connecting your container namespace to the default network namespace.

In a second terminal window, as root, you can create a virtual Ethernet pair by specifying the anonymous namespaces associated with their process IDs, like this:

```
root@myhost:~$ ip link add ve1 netns 28586 type veth peer name ve2 netns 1
```

- `ip link add` indicates that you want to add a link.
- `ve1` is the name of one "end" of the virtual Ethernet "cable."
- `netns 28586` says that this end is "plugged in" to the network namespace associated with process ID 28586 (which is shown in the output from `lsns -t net` in the example at the start of this section).
- `type veth` shows that this a virtual Ethernet pair.
- `peer name ve2` gives the name of the other end of the "cable."
- `netns 1` specifies that this second end is "plugged in" to the network namespace associated with process ID 1.

The `ve1` virtual Ethernet interface is now visible from inside the "container" process:

```
root@myhost:~$ ip a
1: lo: <LOOPBACK> mtu 65536 qdisc noop state DOWN group default qlen 1000
    link/loopback 00:00:00:00:00:00 brd 00:00:00:00:00:00
2: ve1@if3: <BROADCAST,MULTICAST> mtu 1500 qdisc noop state DOWN group ...
    link/ether 7a:8a:3f:ba:61:2c brd ff:ff:ff:ff:ff:ff link-netnsid 0
```

The link is in "DOWN" state and needs to be brought up before it's any use. Both ends of the connection need to be brought up.

Bring up the ve2 end on the host:

```
root@myhost:~$ ip link set ve2 up
```

And once you bring up the ve1 end in the container, the link should move to "UP" state:

```
root@myhost:~$ ip link set ve1 up
root@myhost:~$ ip a
1: lo: <LOOPBACK> mtu 65536 qdisc noop state DOWN group default qlen 1000
    link/loopback 00:00:00:00:00:00 brd 00:00:00:00:00:00
2: ve1@if3: <BROADCAST,MULTICAST,UP,LOWER_UP> mtu 1500 qdisc noqueue state UP ...
    link/ether 7a:8a:3f:ba:61:2c brd ff:ff:ff:ff:ff:ff link-netnsid 0
    inet6 fe80::788a:3fff:feba:612c/64 scope link
        valid_lft forever preferred_lft forever
```

To send IP traffic, there needs to an IP address associated with its interface. In the container:

```
root@myhost:~$ ip addr add 192.168.1.100/24 dev ve1
```

And on the host:

```
root@myhost:~$ ip addr add 192.168.1.200/24 dev ve1
```

This will also have the effect of adding an IP route into the routing table in the container:

```
root@myhost:~$ ip route
192.168.1.0/24 dev ve1 proto kernel scope link src 192.168.1.100
```

As mentioned at the start of this section, the network namespace isolates both the interfaces and the routing table, so this routing information is independent of the IP routing table on the host. At this point the container can send traffic only to 192.168.1.0/24 addresses. You can test this with a ping from within the container to the remote end:

```
root@myhost:~$ ping 192.168.1.100
PING 192.168.1.100 (192.168.1.100) 56(84) bytes of data.
64 bytes from 192.168.1.100: icmp_seq=1 ttl=64 time=0.355 ms
64 bytes from 192.168.1.100: icmp_seq=2 ttl=64 time=0.035 ms
^C
```

We will dig further into networking and container network security in Chapter 10.

User Namespace

The user namespace allows processes to have their own view of user and group IDs. Much like process IDs, the users and groups still exist on the host, but they can have different IDs. The main benefit of this is that you can map the root ID of 0 within a container to some other non-root identity on the host. This is a huge advantage from a security perspective, since it allows software to run as root inside a container, but an attacker who escapes from the container to the host will have a non-root, unprivileged identity. As you'll see in Chapter 9, it's not hard to misconfigure a container to make it easy escape to the host. With user namespaces, you're not just one false move away from host takeover.

 As of this writing, user namespaces are not in particularly common use yet. This feature is not turned on by default in Docker (see "User Namespace Restrictions in Docker" on page 48), and it is not supported at all in Kubernetes, though it has been under discussion (*https://oreil.ly/YBN-i*).

Generally speaking, you need to be root to create new namespaces, which is why the Docker daemon runs as root, but the user namespace is an exception:

```
vagrant@myhost:~$ unshare --user bash
nobody@myhost:~$ id
uid=65534(nobody) gid=65534(nogroup) groups=65534(nogroup)
nobody@myhost:~$ echo $$
31196
```

Inside the new user namespace the user has the nobody ID. You need to put in place a mapping between user IDs inside and outside the namespace, as shown in Figure 4-2.

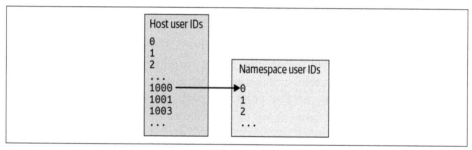

Figure 4-2. Mapping a non-root user on the host to root in a container

This mapping exists in /proc/<pid>/uid_map, which you can edit as root (on the host). There are three fields in this file:

- The lowest ID to map from the child process's perspective
- The lowest corresponding ID that this should map to on the host
- The number of IDs to be mapped

As an example, on my machine, the vagrant user has ID 1000. In order to have vagrant get assigned the root ID of 0 inside the child process, the first two fields are 0 and 1000. The last field can be 1 if you want to map only one ID (which may well be the case if you want only one user inside the container). Here's the command I used to set up that mapping:

```
vagrant@myhost:~$ sudo echo '0 1000 1' > /proc/31196/uid_map
```

Immediately, inside its user namespace, the process has taken on the root identity. Don't be put off by the fact that the bash prompt still says "nobody"; this doesn't get updated unless you rerun the scripts that get run when you start a new shell (e.g., ~/.bash_profile):

```
nobody@myhost:~$ id
uid=0(root) gid=65534(nogroup) groups=65534(nogroup)
```

A similar mapping process is used to map the group(s) used inside the child process.

This process is now running with a large set of capabilities:

```
nobody@myhost:~$ capsh --print | grep Current
Current: = cap_chown,cap_dac_override,cap_dac_read_search,cap_fowner,cap_fsetid,
cap_kill,cap_setgid,cap_setuid,cap_setpcap,cap_linux_immutable,
cap_net_bind_service,cap_net_broadcast,cap_net_admin,cap_net_raw,cap_ipc_lock,
cap_ipc_owner,cap_sys_module,cap_sys_rawio,cap_sys_chroot,cap_sys_ptrace,
cap_sys_pacct,cap_sys_admin,cap_sys_boot,cap_sys_nice,cap_sys_resource,
cap_sys_time,cap_sys_tty_config,cap_mknod,cap_lease,cap_audit_write,
cap_audit_control,cap_setfcap,cap_mac_override,cap_mac_admin,cap_syslog,
cap_wake_alarm,cap_block_suspend,cap_audit_read+ep
```

As you saw in Chapter 2, capabilities grant the process various permissions. When you create a new user namespace, the kernel gives the process all these capabilities so that the pseudo root user inside the namespace is allowed to create other namespaces, set up networking, and so on, fulfilling everything else required to make it a real container.

In fact, if you simultaneously create a process with several new namespaces, the user namespace will be created first so that you have the full capability set that permits you to create other namespaces:

```
vagrant@myhost:~$ unshare --uts bash
unshare: unshare failed: Operation not permitted
vagrant@myhost:~$ unshare --uts --user bash
nobody@myhost:~$
```

User namespaces allow an unprivileged user to effectively become root within the containerized process. This allows a normal user to run containers using a concept called *rootless containers*, which we will cover in Chapter 9.

The general consensus is that user namespaces are a security benefit because fewer containers need to run as "real" root (that is, root from the erspective). However, there have been a few vulnerabilities (for example, CVE-2018-18955 (*https://oreil.ly/ 764Ia*)) directly related to privileges being incorrectly transformed while transitioning to or from a user namespace. The Linux kernel is a complex piece of software, and you should expect that people will find problems in it from time to time.

User Namespace Restrictions in Docker

You can enable the use of user namespaces in Docker, but it's not turned on by default because it is incompatible with a few things that Docker users might want to do.

The following will also affect you if you use user namespaces with other container runtimes:

- User namespaces are incompatible with sharing a process ID or network namespace with the host.

- Even if the process is running as root inside the container, it doesn't really have full root privileges. It doesn't, for example, have CAP_NET_BIND_SERVICE, so it can't bind to a low-numbered port. (See Chapter 2 for more information about Linux capabilities.)

- When the containerized process interacts with a file, it will need appropriate permissions (for example, write access in order to modify the file). If the file is mounted from the host, it is the effective user ID on the host that matters.

  This is a good thing in terms of protecting the host files from unauthorized access from within a container, but it can be confusing if, say, what appears to be root inside the container is not permitted to modify a file.

Inter-process Communications Namespace

In Linux it's possible to communicate between different processes by giving them access to a shared range of memory, or by using a shared message queue. The two processes need to be members of the same inter-process communications (IPC) namespace for them to have access to the same set of identifiers for these mechanisms.

Generally speaking, you *don't* want your containers to be able to access one another's shared memory, so they are given their own IPC namespaces.

You can see this in action by creating a shared memory block and then viewing the current IPC status with ipcs:

```
$ ipcmk -M 1000
Shared memory id: 98307
$ ipcs

------ Message Queues --------
key         msqid      owner      perms      used-bytes   messages
```

```
------ Shared Memory Segments --------
key         shmid     owner     perms     bytes     nattch     status
0x00000000 0          root      644       80        2
0x00000000 32769      root      644       16384     2
0x00000000 65538      root      644       280       2
0xad291bee 98307      ubuntu    644       1000      0

------ Semaphore Arrays --------
key         semid     owner     perms     nsems
0x000000a7 0          root      600       1
```

In this example, the newly created shared memory block (with its ID in the `shmid` column) appears as the last item in the "Shared Memory Segments" block. There are also some preexisting IPC objects that had previously been created by root.

A process with its own IPC namespace does not see any of these IPC objects:

```
$ sudo unshare --ipc sh
$ ipcs

------ Message Queues --------
key         msqid     owner     perms     used-bytes     messages

------ Shared Memory Segments --------
key         shmid     owner     perms     bytes     nattch     status

------ Semaphore Arrays --------
key         semid     owner     perms     nsems
```

Cgroup Namespace

The last of the namespaces (at least, at the time of writing this book) is the cgroup namespace. This is a little bit like a chroot for the cgroup filesystem; it stops a process from seeing the cgroup configuration higher up in the hierarchy of cgroup directories than its own cgroup.

 Most namespaces were added by Linux kernel version 3.8, but the cgroup namespace was added later in version 4.6. If you're using a relatively old distribution of Linux (such as Ubuntu 16.04), you won't have support for this feature. You can check the kernel version on your Linux host by running `uname -r`.

You can see the cgroup namespace in action by comparing the contents of /proc/self/cgroup outside and then inside a cgroup namespace:

```
vagrant@myhost:~$ cat /proc/self/cgroup
12:cpu,cpuacct:/
11:cpuset:/
```

```
10:hugetlb:/
9:blkio:/
8:memory:/user.slice/user-1000.slice/session-51.scope
7:pids:/user.slice/user-1000.slice/session-51.scope
6:freezer:/
5:devices:/user.slice
4:net_cls,net_prio:/
3:rdma:/
2:perf_event:/
1:name=systemd:/user.slice/user-1000.slice/session-51.scope
0::/user.slice/user-1000.slice/session-51.scope
vagrant@myhost:~$
vagrant@myhost:~$ sudo unshare --cgroup bash
root@myhost:~# cat /proc/self/cgroup
12:cpu,cpuacct:/
11:cpuset:/
10:hugetlb:/
9:blkio:/
8:memory:/
7:pids:/
6:freezer:/
5:devices:/
4:net_cls,net_prio:/
3:rdma:/
2:perf_event:/
1:name=systemd:/
0::/
```

You have now explored all the different types of namespace and have seen how they are used along with chroot to isolate a process's view of its surrounding. Combine this with what you learned about cgroups in the previous chapter, and you should have a good understanding of everything that's needed to make what we call a "container."

Before moving on to the next chapter, it's worth taking a look at a container from the perspective of the host it's running on.

Container Processes from the Host Perspective

Although they are called containers, it might be more accurate to use the term "containerized processes." A container is still a Linux process running on the host machine, but it has a limited view of that host machine, and it has access to only a subtree of the filesystem and perhaps to a limited set of resources restricted by cgroups. Because it's really just a process, it exists within the context of the host operating system, and it shares the host's kernel as shown in Figure 4-3.

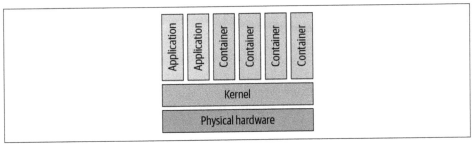

Figure 4-3. Containers share the host's kernel

You'll see how this compares to virtual machines in the next chapter, but before that, let's examine in more detail the extent to which a containerized process is isolated from the host, and from other containerized processes on that host, by trying some experiments on a Docker container. Start a container process based on Ubuntu (or your favorite Linux distribution) and run a shell in it, and then run a long sleep in it as follows:

```
$ docker run --rm -it ubuntu bash
root@1551d24a $ sleep 1000
```

This example runs the sleep command for 1,000 seconds, but note that the sleep command is running as a process inside the container. When you press Enter at the end of the sleep command, this triggers Linux to clone a new process with a new process ID and to run the sleep executable within that process.

You can put the sleep process into the background (Ctrl-Z to pause the process, and bg %1 to background it). Now run ps inside the container to see the same process from the container's perspective:

```
me@myhost:~$ docker run --rm -it ubuntu bash
root@ab6ea36fce8e:/$ sleep 1000
^Z
[1]+  Stopped                 sleep 1000
root@ab6ea36fce8e:/$ bg %1
[1]+ sleep 1000 &
root@ab6ea36fce8e:/$ ps
  PID TTY          TIME CMD
    1 pts/0    00:00:00 bash
   10 pts/0    00:00:00 sleep
   11 pts/0    00:00:00 ps
root@ab6ea36fce8e:/$
```

While that sleep command is still running, open a second terminal into the same host and look at the same sleep process from the host's perspective:

```
me@myhost:~$ ps -C sleep
  PID TTY          TIME CMD
30591 pts/0    00:00:00 sleep
```

The `-C sleep` parameter specifies that we are interested only in processes running the `sleep` executable.

The container has its own process ID namespace, so it makes sense that its processes would have low numbers, and that is indeed what you see when running ps in the container. From the host's perspective, however, the sleep process has a different, high-numbered process ID. In the preceding example, there is just one process, and it has ID 30591 on the host and 10 in the container. (The actual number will vary according to what else is and has been running on the same machine, but it's likely to be a much higher number.)

To get a good understanding of containers and the level of isolation they provide, it's really key to get to grips with the fact that although there are two different process IDs, they both refer to *the same process*. It's just that from the host's perspective it has a higher process ID number.

The fact that container processes are visible from the host is one of the fundamental differences between containers and virtual machines. An attacker who gets access to the host can observe and affect *all the containers running on that host*, especially if they have root access. And as you'll see in Chapter 9, there are some remarkably easy ways you can inadvertently make it possible for an attacker to move from a compromised container onto the host.

Container Host Machines

As you have seen, containers and their host share a kernel, and this has some consequences for what are considered best practices relating to the host machines for containers. If a host gets compromised, all the containers on that host are potential victims, especially if the attacker gains root or otherwise elevated privileges (such as being a member of the docker group that can administer containers where Docker is used as the runtime).

It's highly recommended to run container applications on dedicated host machines (whether they be VMs or bare metal), and the reasons mostly relate to security:

- Using an orchestrator to run containers means that humans need little or no access to the hosts. If you don't run any other applications, you will need a very small set of user identities on the host machines. These will be easier to manage, and attempts to log in as an unauthorized user will be easier to spot.

- You can use any Linux distribution as the host OS for running Linux containers, but there are several "Thin OS" distros specifically designed for running containers. These reduce the host attack surface by including only the components required to run containers. Examples include RancherOS, Red Hat's Fedora CoreOS, and VMware's Photon OS. With fewer components included in the host machine, there is a smaller chance of vulnerabilities (see Chapter 7) in those components.

- All the host machines in a cluster can share the same configuration, with no application-specific requirements. This makes it easy to automate the provisioning of host machines, and it means you can treat host machines as immutable. If a host machine needs an upgrade, you don't patch it; instead, you remove it from the cluster and replace it with a freshly installed machine. Treating hosts as immutable makes intrusions easier to detect.

I'll come back to the advantages of immutability in Chapter 6.

Using a Thin OS reduces the set of configuration options but doesn't eliminate them completely. For example, you will have a container runtime (perhaps Docker) plus orchestrator code (perhaps the Kubernetes kubelet) running on every host. These components have numerous settings, some of which affect security. The Center for Internet Security (*https://cisecurity.org*) (CIS) publishes benchmarks for best practices for configuring and running various software components, including Docker, Kubernetes, and Linux.

In an enterprise environment, look for a container security solution that also protects the hosts by reporting on vulnerabilities and worrisome configuration settings. You will also want logs and alerts for logins and login attempts at the host level.

Summary

Congratulations! Since you've reached the end of this chapter, you should now know what a container really is. You've seen the three essential Linux kernel mechanisms that are used to limit a process's access to host resources:

- Namespaces limit what the container process can see—for example, by giving the container an isolated set of process IDs.
- Changing the root limits the set of files and directories that the container can see.
- Cgroups control the resources the container can access.

As you saw in Chapter 1, isolating one workload from another is an important aspect of container security. You now should be fully aware that all the containers on a given host (whether it is a virtual machine or a bare-metal server) share the same kernel. Of course, the same is true in a multiuser system where different users can log in to the same machine and run applications directly. However, in a multiuser system, the administrators are likely to limit the permissions given to each user; they certainly won't give them all root privileges. With containers—at least at the time of writing— they all run as root by default and are relying on the boundary provided by namespaces, changed root directories, and cgroups to prevent one container from interfering with another.

> Now that you know how containers work, you might want to explore Jess Frazelle's contained.af site to see just how effective they are. Will you be the person who breaks the containment?

In Chapter 8 we'll explore options for strengthening the security boundary around each container, but next let's delve into how virtual machines work. This will allow you to consider the relative strengths of the isolation between containers and between VMs, especially through the lens of security.

CHAPTER 5

Virtual Machines

Containers are often compared with virtual machines (VMs), especially in terms of the isolation that they offer. Let's make sure you have a solid understanding of how VMs operate so that you can reason about the differences between them and containers. This will be particularly useful when you want to assess the security boundaries around your applications when they run in containers, or in different VMs. When you are discussing the relative merits of containers from a security perspective, understanding how they differ from VMs can be a useful tool.

This isn't a black-and-white distinction, really. As you'll see in Chapter 8, there are several sandboxing tools that strengthen the isolation boundaries around containers, making them more like VMs. If you want to understand the security pros and cons of these approaches, it's best to start with a firm understanding of the difference between a VM and a "normal" container.

The fundamental difference is that a VM runs an entire copy of an operating system, including its kernel, whereas a container shares the host machine's kernel. To understand what that means, you'll need to know something about how virtual machines are created and managed by a Virtual Machine Monitor (VMM). Let's start to set the scene for that by thinking about what happens when a computer boots up.

Booting Up a Machine

Picture a physical server. It has some CPUs, memory, and networking interfaces. When you first boot up the machine, an initial program runs that's called the BIOS, or Basic Input Output System. It scans how much memory is available, identifies the network interfaces, and spots any other devices such as displays, keyboards, attached storage devices, and so on.

In practice, a lot of this functionality has been superseded nowadays by UEFI (Unified Extensible Firmware Interface), but for the sake of argument, let's just think of this as a modern BIOS.

Once the hardware has been enumerated, the system runs a bootloader that loads and then runs the operating system's kernel code. The operating system could be Linux, Windows, or some other OS. As you saw in Chapter 2, kernel code operates at a higher level of privilege than your application code. This privilege level allows it to interact with memory, network interfaces, and so on, whereas applications running in user space can't do this directly.

On an x86 processor, privilege levels are organized into *rings*, with Ring 0 being the most privileged and Ring 3 being the least privileged. For most operating systems in a regular setup (without VMs), the kernel runs at Ring 0 and user space code runs at Ring 3, as shown in Figure 5-1.

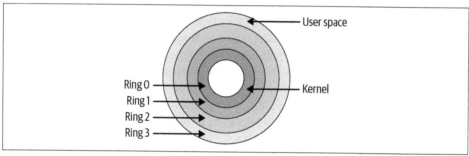

Figure 5-1. Privilege rings

Kernel code (like any code) runs on the CPU in the form of machine code instructions, and these instructions can include privileged instructions for accessing memory, starting CPU threads, and so on. The details of everything that can and will happen while the kernel initializes are beyond the scope of this book, but essentially the goal is to mount the root filesystem, set up networking, and bring up any system daemons. (If you want to dive deeper, there is a lot of great information on Linux kernel internals, including the bootstrap process, on GitHub (*https://oreil.ly/GPutF*).)

Once the kernel has finished its own initialization, it can start running programs in user space. The kernel is responsible for managing everything that the user space programs need. It starts, manages, and schedules the CPU threads that these programs run in, and it keeps track of these threads through its own data structures that represent processes. One important aspect of kernel functionality is memory management. The kernel assigns blocks of memory to each process and makes sure that processes can't access one another's memory blocks.

Enter the VMM

As you have just seen, in a regular setup, the kernel manages the machine's resources directly. In the world of virtual machines, a Virtual Machine Monitor (VMM) does the first layer of resource management, splitting up the resources and assigning them to virtual machines. Each virtual machine gets a kernel of its own.

For each virtual machine that it manages, the VMM assigns some memory and CPU resources, sets up some virtual network interfaces and other virtual devices, and starts a guest kernel with access to these resources.

In a regular server, the BIOS gives the kernel the details of the resources available on the machine; in a virtual machine situation, the VMM divides up those resources and gives each guest kernel only the details of the subset that it is being given access to. From the perspective of the guest OS, it thinks it has direct access to physical memory and devices, but in fact it's getting access to an abstraction provided by the VMM.

The VMM is responsible for making sure that the guest OS and its applications can't breach the boundaries of the resources it has been allocated. For example, the guest operating system is assigned a range of memory on the host machine. If the guest somehow tries to access memory outside that range, this is forbidden.

There are two main forms of VMM, often called, not very imaginatively, Type 1 and Type 2. And there is a bit of gray area between the two, naturally!

Type 1 VMMs, or Hypervisors

In a regular system, the bootloader runs an operating system kernel like Linux or Windows. In a pure Type 1 virtual machine environment, a dedicated kernel-level VMM program runs instead.

Type 1 VMMs are also known as *hypervisors*, and examples include Hyper-V (*https://oreil.ly/FsXVi*), Xen (*https://xenproject.org/*), and ESX/ESXi (*https://oreil.ly/ezG3t*). As you can see in Figure 5-2, the hypervisor runs directly on the hardware (or "bare metal"), with no operating system underneath it.

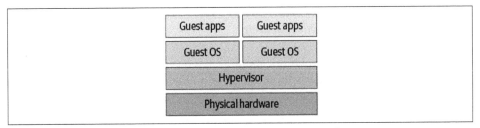

Figure 5-2. Type 1 Virtual Machine Monitor, also known as a hypervisor

In saying "kernel level," I mean that the hypervisor runs at Ring 0. (Well, that's true until we consider hardware virtualization later in this chapter, but for now let's just assume Ring 0.) The guest OS kernel runs at Ring 1, as depicted in Figure 5-3, which means it has less privilege than the hypervisor.

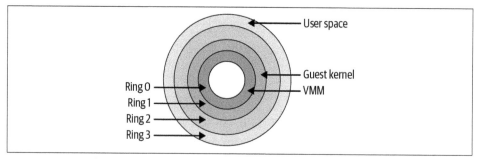

Figure 5-3. Privilege rings used under a hypervisor

Type 2 VMM

When you run virtual machines on your laptop or desktop machine, perhaps through something like VirtualBox (*https://www.virtualbox.org*), they are "hosted" or Type 2 VMs. Your laptop might be running, say, macOS, which is to say that it's running a macOS kernel. You install VirtualBox as a separate application, which then goes on to manage guest VMs that coexist with your host operating system. Those guest VMs could be running Linux or Windows. Figure 5-4 shows how the guest OS and host OS coexist.

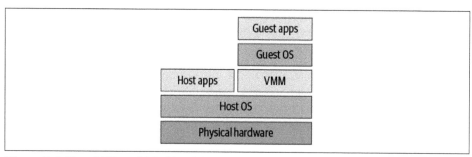

Figure 5-4. Type 2 Virtual Machine Monitor

Consider that for a moment and think about what it means to run, say, Linux within a macOS. By definition this means there has to be a Linux kernel, and that has to be a different kernel from the host's macOS kernel.

The VMM application has user space components that you can interact with as a user, but it also installs privileged components allowing it to provide virtualization. You'll see more about how this works later in this chapter.

Besides VirtualBox, other examples of Type 2 VMMs include Parallels (*https://paral lels.com*) and QEMU (*https://oreil.ly/LZmcn*).

Kernel-Based Virtual Machines

I promised that there would be some blurred boundaries between Type 1 and Type 2. In Type 1, the hypervisor runs directly on bare metal; in Type 2, the VMM runs in user space on the host OS. What if you run a virtual machine manager within the kernel of the host OS?

This is exactly what happens with a Linux kernel module called KVM, or Kernel-based Virtual Machines, as shown in Figure 5-5.

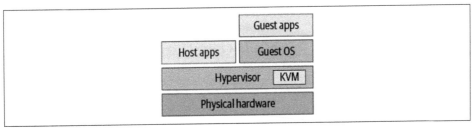

Figure 5-5. KVM

Generally, KVM is considered to be a Type 1 hypervisor because the guest OS doesn't have to traverse the host OS, but I'd say that this categorization is overly simplistic.

KVM is often used with QEMU (Quick Emulation), which I listed earlier as a Type 2 hypervisor. QEMU dynamically translates system calls from the guest OS into host OS system calls. It's worth a mention that QEMU can take advantage of hardware acceleration offered by KVM.

Whether Type 1, Type 2, or something in between, VMMs employ similar techniques to achieve virtualization. The basic idea is called "trap-and-emulate," though as we'll see, x86 processors provide some challenges in implementing this idea.

Trap-and-Emulate

Some CPU instructions are *privileged*, meaning they can be executed only in Ring 0; if they are attempted in a higher ring, this will cause a *trap*. You can think of the trap as being like an exception in application software that triggers an error handler; a trap will result in the CPU calling to a handler in the Ring 0 code.

If the VMM runs at Ring 0 and the guest OS kernel code runs at a lower privilege, a privileged instruction run by the guest can invoke a handler in the VMM to emulate the instruction. In this way the VMM can ensure that the guest OSs can't interfere with each other through privileged instructions.

Unfortunately, privileged instructions are only part of the story. The set of CPU instructions that can affect the machine's resources is known as *sensitive*. The VMM needs to handle these instructions on behalf of the guest OS, because only the VMM has a true view of the machine's resources. There is also another class of sensitive instructions that behaves differently when executed in Ring 0 or in lower-privileged rings. Again, a VMM needs to do something about these instructions because the guest OS code was written assuming the Ring 0 behavior.

If all sensitive instructions were privileged, this would make life relatively easy for VMM programmers, as they would just need to write trap handlers for all these sensitive instructions. Unfortunately, not all x86 sensitive instructions are also privileged, so VMMs need to use different techniques to handle them. Instructions that are sensitive but not privileged are considered to be "non-virtualizable."

Handling Non-Virtualizable Instructions

There are a few different techniques for handling these non-virtualizable instructions:

- One option is *binary translation*. All the non-privileged, sensitive instructions in the guest OS are spotted and rewritten by the VMM in real time. This is complex, and newer x86 processors support hardware-assisted virtualization to simplify binary translation.

- Another option is *paravirtualization*. Instead of modifying the guest OS on the fly, the guest OS is rewritten to avoid the non-virtualizable set of instructions, effectively making system calls to the hypervisor. This is the technique used by the Xen hypervisor.

- Hardware virtualization (such as Intel's VT-x) allows hypervisors to run in a new, extra privileged level known as *VMX root mode*, which is essentially Ring –1. This allows the VM guest OS kernels to run at Ring 0 (or VMX non-root mode), as they would if they were the host OS.

 If you would like to dig deeper into how virtualization works, Keith Adams and Ole Agesen (*https://oreil.ly/D1cZO*) provide a useful comparison and describe how hardware enhancements enable better performance.

Now that you have a picture of how virtual machines are created and managed, let's consider what this means in terms of isolating one process, or application, from another.

Process Isolation and Security

Making sure that applications are safely isolated from each other is a primary security concern. If my application can read the memory that belongs to your application, I will have access to your data.

Physical isolation is the strongest form of isolation possible. If our applications are running on entirely separate physical machines, there is no way for my code to get access to the memory of your application.

As we have just discussed, the kernel is responsible for managing its user space processes, including assigning memory to each process. It's up to the kernel to make sure that one application can't access the memory assigned to another. If there is a bug in the way that the kernel manages memory, an attacker might be able to exploit that bug to access memory that they shouldn't be able to reach. And while the kernel is extremely battle-tested, it's also extremely large and complex, and it is still evolving. Even though we don't know of significant flaws in kernel isolation as of this writing, I wouldn't advise you to bet against someone finding problems at some point in the future.

These flaws can come about due to increased sophistication in the underlying hardware. In recent years, CPU manufacturers developed "speculative processing," in which a processor runs ahead of the currently executing instruction and works out what the results are going to be ahead of actually needing to run that branch of code. This enabled significant performance gains, but it also opened the door to the famous Spectre and Meltdown exploits.

You might be wondering why people consider hypervisors to give greater isolation to virtual machines than a kernel gives to its processes; after all, hypervisors are also managing memory and device access and have a responsibility to keep virtual machines separate. It's absolutely true that a hypervisor flaw could result in a serious problem with isolation between virtual machines. The difference is that hypervisors have a much, much simpler job. In a kernel, user space processes are allowed some visibility of each other; as a very simple example, you can run ps and see the running processes on the same machine. You can (given the right permissions) access information about those processes by looking in the /proc directory. You are allowed to deliberately share memory between processes through IPC and, well, shared memory. All these mechanisms, where one process is legitimately allowed to discover information about another, make the isolation weaker, because of the possibility of a flaw that allows this access in unexpected or unintended circumstances.

There is no similar equivalent when running virtual machines; you can't see one machine's processes from another. There is less code required to manage memory simply because the hypervisor doesn't need to handle circumstances in which machines might share memory—it's just not something that virtual machines do. As a result, hypervisors are far smaller and simpler than full kernels. There are well over 20 million lines of code in the Linux kernel (*https://oreil.ly/FHKhp*); by contrast, the Xen hypervisor is around 50,000 lines (*https://oreil.ly/1MWub*).

Where there is less code and less complexity, there is a smaller attack surface, and the likelihood of an exploitable flaw is less. For this reason, virtual machines are considered to have strong isolation boundaries.

That said, virtual machine exploits are not unheard of. Darshan Tank, Akshai Aggarwal, and Nirbhay Chaubey (*https://oreil.ly/HCXBO*) describe a taxonomy of the different types of attack, and the National Institute of Standards and Technology (NIST) has published security guidelines (*https://oreil.ly/W_b7o*) for hardening virtualized environments.

Disadvantages of Virtual Machines

At this point you might be so convinced of the isolation advantages of virtual machines that you might be wondering why people use containers at all! There are some disadvantages of VMs compared to containers:

- Virtual machines have start-up times that are several orders of magnitude greater than a container. After all, a container simply means starting a new Linux process, not having to go through the whole start-up and initialization of a VM. The relatively slow start-up times of VMs means that they are sluggish for autoscaling, not to mention that fast start-up times are important when an organization wants to ship new code frequently, perhaps several times per day. (However, Amazon's Firecracker, discussed in "Firecracker" on page 103, offers VMs with very fast start-up times, of the order of 100ms as of this writing.)

- Containers give developers a convenient ability to "build once, run anywhere" quickly and efficiently. It's possible, but very slow, to build an entire machine image for a VM and run it on one's laptop, but this technique hasn't taken off in the developer community in the way containers have.

- In today's cloud environments, when you rent a virtual machine you have to specify its CPU and memory, and you pay for those resources regardless of how much is actually used by the application code running inside it.

- Each virtual machine has the overhead of running a whole kernel. By sharing a kernel, containers can be very efficient in both resource use and performance.

When choosing whether to use VMs or containers, there are many trade-offs to be made among factors such as performance, price, convenience, risk, and the strength of security boundary required between different application workloads.

Container Isolation Compared to VM Isolation

As you saw in Chapter 4, containers are simply Linux processes with a restricted view. They are isolated from each other by the kernel through the mechanisms of namespaces, cgroups, and changing the root. These mechanisms were created specifically to create isolation between processes. However, the simple fact that containers share a kernel means that the basic isolation is weaker compared to that of VMs.

However, all is not lost! You can apply additional security features and sandboxing to strengthen this isolation, which I will explain in Chapter 8. There are also very effective security tools that take advantage of the fact that containers tend to encapsulate microservices, and I will cover these in Chapter 13.

Summary

You should now have a good grasp of what virtual machines are. You have learned why the isolation between virtual machines is considered strong compared to container isolation, and why containers are generally not considered suitably secure for hard multitenancy environments. Understanding this difference is an important tool to have in your toolbox when discussing container security.

Securing virtual machines themselves is outside the scope of this book, although I touched on hardening container host configuration in "Container Host Machines" on page 52.

Later in this book you will see some examples in which the weaker isolation of containers (in comparison to VMs) can easily be broken through misconfiguration. Before we get to that, let's make sure you are up to speed on what's inside a container image and how images can have a significant bearing on security.

CHAPTER 6

Container Images

If you have been using Docker or Kubernetes, you are likely to be familiar with the idea of container images that you store in a registry. In this chapter we're going to explore container images, looking at what they contain and how container runtimes like Docker or runc use them.

With an understanding of what images are under your belt, you're ready to think about the security implications of building, storing, and retrieving images—and there are a lot of attack vectors related to these steps. You'll learn about best practices for ensuring that builds and images don't compromise your overall system.

Root Filesystem and Image Configuration

There are two parts to a container image: the root filesystem and some configuration.

If you followed along with the examples in Chapter 4, you downloaded a copy of the Alpine root filesystem and used this as the contents of root inside your container. In general, when you start a container you instantiate it from a container image, and the image includes the root filesystem. If you run docker run -it alpine sh and compare it to what's inside your hand-built container, you will see the same layout of directories and files, and they will match completely if the version of Alpine is the same.

If, like many people, you have come to containers through the use of Docker, you'll be used to the idea of building images based on the instructions in a Dockerfile. Some Dockerfile commands (like FROM, ADD, COPY, or RUN) modify the contents of the root filesystem that's included in the image. Other commands, like USER, PORT, or ENV, affect the configuration information that's stored in the image alongside the root filesystem. You can see this config information by running docker inspect on an image. This config information gives Docker instructions on runtime parameters that should be set up by default when running the image. For example, if an environment variable is specified using an `ENV` command in the Dockerfile, this environment variable will be defined for the container process when it runs.

Overriding Config at Runtime

In Docker, the config information can be overridden at runtime using command-line parameters. For example, if you want to change an environment variable or set a new one, you can do this with `docker run -e <VARNAME>=<NEWVALUE> ....`

In Kubernetes, you do this with an `env` definition for the container in a pod's YAML definition:

```
apiVersion: v1
kind: Pod
metadata:
  name: demo
spec:
  containers:
  - name: demo-container
    image: demo-reg.io/some-org/demo-image:1.0
    env:
    - name: DEMO_ENV
      value: "This overrides the value"
```

The (imaginary) image `demo-image:1.0` was built from a Dockerfile, which might have included the line `ENV DEMO_ENV="The original value"`. This YAML overrides the value for `DEMO_ENV`, and if the container were to log the value of this variable, you would see `This overrides the value`.

If the container runtime in your Kubernetes deployment is an OCI-compliant tool like `runc`, the values from the YAML definition end up in an OCI-compliant con fig.json file. Let's find out more about these OCI standard container files and tools.

OCI Standards

The Open Container Initiative (*https://opencontainers.org*) (OCI) was formed to define standards around container images and runtime. It took its lead from a lot of the work that had been done in Docker, so there is quite a lot in common between what happens in Docker and what is defined in the specs—in particular, a goal of the OCI was for the standards to support the same user experience that Docker users had come to expect, like the ability to run an image with a default set of configuration settings. The OCI specs cover an image format, which discusses how container images are built and distributed.

Skopeo (*https://oreil.ly/Rxejf*) is useful for manipulating and inspecting OCI images. It can generate an OCI-format image from a Docker image:

```
$ skopeo copy docker://alpine:latest oci:alpine:latest
$ ls alpine
blobs  index.json  oci-layout
```

But an OCI-compliant runtime like runc doesn't work directly with the image in this format. Instead, it first has to be unpacked into a runtime *filesystem bundle* (*https://oreil.ly/VtJ0F*). Let's look at an example, using umoci (*https://oreil.ly/Rdfab*) to unpack the image:

```
$ sudo umoci unpack --image alpine:latest alpine-bundle
$ ls alpine-bundle
config.json
rootfs
sha256_3bf9de52f38aa287b5793bd2abca9bca62eb097ad06be660bfd78927c1395651.mtree
umoci.json
$ ls alpine-bundle/rootfs
bin  etc  lib   mnt  proc  run   srv  tmp  var
dev  home media  opt  root  sbin  sys  usr
```

As you can see, this bundle includes a rootfs directory with the contents of an Alpine Linux distribution. There is also a *config.json* file that defines the runtime settings. The runtime instantiates a container using this root filesystem and settings.

When you're using Docker, you don't get direct access to the config information in the form of a file you can inspect with cat or your favorite text editor, but you can see that it's there by using the docker image inspect command.

Image Configuration

Now that you know from Chapters 3 and 4 how containers are created, it's worth taking a look at one of these *config.json* files, because a lot of it should look familiar. Here's an extract as an example:

```
...
    "linux": {
        "resources": {
            "memory": {
                "limit": 1000000
            },
            "devices": [
                {
                    "allow": false,
                    "access": "rwm"
                }
            ]
        },
        "namespaces": [
            {
                "type": "pid"
            },
```

```
            {
                    "type": "network"
            },
            {
                    "type": "ipc"
            },
            {
                    "type": "uts"
            },
            {
                    "type": "mount"
            }
        ]
    }
```

As you can see, the configuration information includes a definition of everything runc should do to create the container, including a list of any resources that it should constrain through cgroups, and the namespaces it should create.

You have seen how an image consists of two parts: the root filesystem and some configuration information. Now let's consider how an image gets built.

Building Images

Most people's experience of building container images is to use the `docker build` command. This follows the instructions from a file called a Dockerfile to create an image. Before discussing the build itself, I'd like to briefly discuss why `docker build` needs careful attention from a security point of view.

 Docker has been working on a rootless mode that should address the issues described in the upcoming section, but as I write it's still considered "experimental."

The Dangers of docker build

When you run a `docker` command, the command-line tool you invoked (`docker`) does very little by itself. Instead, it converts your command into an API request that it sends to the Docker daemon via a socket referred to as the Docker socket. Any process that has access to the Docker socket can send API requests to the daemon.

The Docker daemon is a long-running process that actually does the work of running and managing both containers and container images. As you saw in Chapter 4, in order to create a container, the daemon needs to be able to create namespaces, so it needs to be running as root.

Imagine that you want to dedicate a machine (or virtual machine) to build container images and store them in a registry. Using the Docker approach, your machine has to run the daemon, which has a lot more capabilities beyond building and interacting with registries. Without additional security tooling, any user who can trigger a `docker build` on this machine can also perform a `docker run` to execute any command they like on the machine.

Not only can they run any command they like, but also, if they use this privilege to perform a malicious action, it will be hard to track down who was responsible. You may keep an audit log of certain actions that users take, but—as illustrated nicely in a post by Dan Walsh (*https://oreil.ly/TszBl*)—the audit will record the daemon process's ID rather than that of the user.

To avoid these security risks, there are several alternative tools for building container images without relying on the Docker daemon.

Daemonless Builds

One such tool is BuildKit (*https://oreil.ly/jefkr*) from the Moby project, which can also run in rootless mode. (As you may know, Docker renamed its open source code "Moby" in an attempt to avoid the inevitable confusion when the project and company names were the same.) BuildKit is a foundation for the experimental Docker rootless build mode noted previously.

Other non-privileged builds include Red Hat's `podman` (*https://podman.io*) and `buildah` (*https://buildah.io*). A blog post from Puja Abbassi (*https://oreil.ly/FNYY_*) describes these tools and compares them to `docker build`.

Google's Bazel (*https://oreil.ly/Jz_30*) can build many other types of artifact, not just container images. Not only does it not require Docker, but it also prides itself on generating images deterministically so that you can reproduce the same image from the same source.

Google also produced a tool called Kaniko (*https://oreil.ly/_nRoM*) for running builds within a Kubernetes cluster without needing access to the Docker daemon.

Other "daemonless" tools for building containers include Jess Frazelle's `img` (*https://oreil.ly/RfXtm*) and Aleksa Sarai's `orca-build` (*https://oreil.ly/kimqz*).

At the time of writing, it's not obvious that there is a clear winner from among any of these tools.

Image Layers

Regardless of which tool you use, the vast majority of container image builds are defined through a Dockerfile. The Dockerfile gives a series of instructions, each of which results in either a filesystem layer or a change to the image configuration. This is described well in the Docker documentation (*https://oreil.ly/zGJpP*), but if you want to dig into the details, you might enjoy the blog post I wrote about re-creating the Dockerfile from an image (*https://oreil.ly/2SSdJ*).

Sensitive data in layers

Anyone who has access to a container image can access any file included in that image. From a security perspective, you want to avoid including sensitive information such as passwords or tokens in an image. (I'll cover how you should handle this information in Chapter 12.)

The fact that every layer is stored separately means that you have to be careful not to store sensitive data, even if a subsequent layer removes it. Here's a Dockerfile that illustrates what *not* to do:

```
FROM alpine
RUN echo "top-secret" > /password.txt
RUN rm /password.txt
```

One layer creates a file, and then the next layer removes it. If you build this image and then run it, you won't find any sign of the *password.txt* file:

```
vagrant@vagrant:~$ docker run --rm -it sensitive ls /password.txt
ls: /password.txt: No such file or directory
```

But don't let this fool you—the sensitive data is still included in the image. You can prove this by exporting the image to a tar file using the docker save command and then unpacking the tar:

```
vagrant@vagrant:~$ docker save sensitive > sensitive.tar
vagrant@vagrant:~$ mkdir sensitive
vagrant@vagrant:~$ cd sensitive
vagrant@vagrant:~$ tar -xf ../sensitive.tar
vagrant@vagrant:~/sensitive$ ls
0c247e34f78415b03155dae3d2ec7ed941801aa8aeb3cb4301eab9519302a3b9.json
552e9f7172fe87f322d421aec2b124691cd80edc9ba3fef842b0564e7a86041e
818c5ec07b8ee1d0d3ed6e12875d9d597c210b488e74667a03a58cd43dc9be1a
8e635d6264340a45901f63d2a18ea5bc8c680919e07191e4ef276860952d0399
manifest.json
```

Inspecting the content will make it pretty clear what each of these files and directories are for:

- manifest.json is the top-level file describing the image. It tells you which file represents the config (the 0c24...json file in this case), describes any tags for this image, and lists each of the layers.

- 0c24...json is the config for the image (as described earlier in this chapter).

- Each of the directories represents one of the layers that make up the root filesystem for the image.

The config includes the history of the commands that were run to construct this container. As you can see, in this case the sensitive data is revealed in the step that runs the echo command:

```
vagrant@vagrant:~/sensitive$ cat 0c247*.json | jq '.history'
[
  {
    "created": "2019-10-21T17:21:42.078618181Z",
    "created_by": "/bin/sh -c #(nop) ADD
    file:fe1f09249227e2da2089afb4d07e16cbf832eeb804120074acd2b8192876cd28 in / "
  },
  {
    "created": "2019-10-21T17:21:42.387111039Z",
    "created_by": "/bin/sh -c #(nop)  CMD [\"/bin/sh\"]",
    "empty_layer": true
  },
  {
    "created": "2019-12-16T13:50:43.9149721682Z",
    "created_by": "/bin/sh -c echo \"top-secret\" > /password.txt"
  },
  {
    "created": "2019-12-16T13:50:45.0853492852Z",
    "created_by": "/bin/sh -c rm /password.txt"
  }
]
```

Inside each layer's directory there is another tar file holding the contents of the filesystem at that layer. It's easy to reveal the *password.txt* file from the appropriate layer:

```
vagrant@vagrant:~/sensitive$ tar -xf 55*/layer.tar
vagrant@vagrant:~/sensitive$ cat password.txt
top-secret
```

As this shows, even if a subsequent layer deletes a file, any file that ever existed in any layer can easily be obtained by unpacking the image. Don't include anything in any layer that you aren't prepared to be seen by anyone who has access to the image.

Earlier in this chapter you saw what's inside an OCI-compliant container image, and you now know what is happening when these images are built from a Dockerfile. Now let's consider how images are stored.

Storing Images

Images are stored in container registries. If you use Docker, you've probably used the Docker Hub (*https://hub.docker.com*) registry, and if you're working with containers using the services of a cloud provider, it's likely you're familiar with one of their registries—Amazon's Elastic Container Registry, for example, or Google Container

Registry. Storing an image in a registry is generally referred to as a *push*, and retrieving it is a *pull*.

At the time of writing, the OCI is working on a distribution specification (*https:// oreil.ly/3Jvl7*) that defines the interface for interacting with a container registry, where containers are stored. Although this is a work in progress, it leans on prior art from these existing container registries.

Each layer is stored separately as a "blob" of data in the registry, identified by a hash of its contents. To save storage space, a given blob needs to be stored only once, although it may be referenced by many images. The registry also stores an image *manifest* that identifies the set of image layer blobs that make up the image. Taking a hash of the image manifest gives a unique identifier for the entire image, which is referred to as the image *digest*. If you rebuild the image and anything about it changes, this hash will also change.

If you're using Docker, you can easily see the digests for images held locally on your machine by using the following command:

```
vagrant@vagrant:~$ docker image ls --digests
REPOSITORY    TAG      DIGEST                IMAGE ID       CREATED       SIZE
nginx         latest   sha256:50cf...8566    231d40e811cd   2 weeks ago   126MB
```

When you push or pull an image, you can use this digest to precisely reference this particular build, but this isn't the only way you can refer to an image. Let's review the different ways of identifying container images.

Identifying Images

The first part of an image reference is the URL of the registry where it is stored. (If the registry address is omitted, this implies either a locally stored image or an image stored on Docker Hub, depending on the command context.)

The next part of an image reference is the name of the user or organization account that owns this image. This is followed by an image name, and then either the digest that identifies its contents or a human-readable tag.

Putting this together gives us an address that looks like one of these options:

```
<Registry URL>/<Organization or user name>/<repository>@sha256:<digest>
<Registry URL>/<Organization or user name>/<repository>:<tag>
```

If the registry URL is omitted, it defaults to Docker Hub's address, `docker.io`. Figure 6-1 shows an example version of an image as it appears on Docker Hub.

You could pull this image with either of the following commands:

```
vagrant@vagrant:~$ docker pull aquasec/trivy:0.2.1
vagrant@vagrant:~$ docker pull aquasec/
trivy:sha256:4c0b03c25c500bce7a1851643ff3c7b774d863a6f7311364b92a450f3a78e6a3
```

Referring to an image by hash is unwieldy for humans to deal with, hence the commonplace use of *tags*, which are just arbitrary labels applied to the image. A single image can be given any number of tags, and the same tag can be moved from one image to another. Tags are often used to indicate the version of software contained in the image—as in the example just shown, which is version 0.2.1.

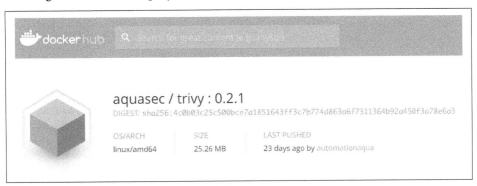

Figure 6-1. Example image on Docker Hub

Because tags can be moved from image to image, there is no guarantee that specifying an image by tag today will give you exactly the same result as it does tomorrow. In contrast, using the hash reference will give you the identical image, because the hash is defined from the contents of the image. Any change to the image results in a different hash.

This effect may be exactly what you intend. For example, you might refer to an image using a tag that refers to the major and minor version number in a semantic versioning schema. If a new patched version is released, you rely on the image maintainers to retag the patched image with the same major and minor version number so that you get the up-to-date patched version when you next pull the image.

However, there are occasions when the unique reference to an image is important. For example, consider the scanning of images for vulnerabilities (which is covered in Chapter 7). You might have an admission controller that checks that images can be deployed only if they have been through the vulnerability scanning step, and this will need to check records of the images that have been scanned. If these records refer to the images by tag, the information is unreliable, as there's no way of knowing whether the image has changed and needs to be rescanned.

Now that you know how images are stored, let's turn to the security concerns that relate to images.

Image Security

The main concern when it comes to image security is image integrity—that is, ensuring that the intended images are what gets used. If an attacker is able to get an unintended image running in a deployment, they can run any code they like. There are various potential weak points in the chain, from building and storing an image to running the image, as shown in Figure 6-2.

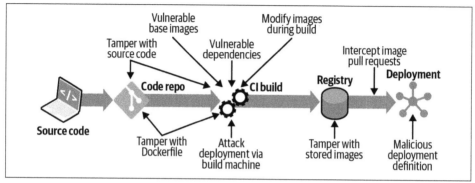

Figure 6-2. Image attack vectors

Application developers can affect security through the code they write. Static and dynamic analysis tools, peer review, and testing can all help to identify insecurities added during development. This all applies for containerized applications just as it does without containers. But since this book is concerned with containers, let's move on to discussing the potential for weaknesses that can be introduced at the point where you build a container image.

Build-Time Security

The build step takes a Dockerfile and converts it into a container image. Within that step, there are a number of potential security risks.

Provenance of the Dockerfile

The instructions for building an image come from a Dockerfile. Each stage of the build involves running one of these instructions, and if a bad actor is able to modify the Dockerfile, it's possible for them to take malicious actions, including:

- adding malware or cryptomining software into the image
- accessing build secrets
- enumerating the network topology accessible from the build infrastructure

- attacking the build host

It may seem obvious, but the Dockerfile (like any source code) needs appropriate access controls to protect against attackers adding malicious steps into the build.

The contents of the Dockerfile also have a huge bearing on the security of the image that the build produces. Let's turn to some practical steps you can take in the Dockerfile to improve image security.

Dockerfile Best Practices for Security

These recommendations all improve the security of the image and reduce the chances that an attacker can compromise containers running from this image:

Base image
> The first line of the Dockerfile is a FROM instruction indicating a base image that the new image is built from.
>
> - Refer to an image from a trusted registry (see "Image Storage Security" on page 77).
> - Arbitrary third-party base images might include malicious code, so some organizations mandate the use of preapproved or "golden" base images.
> - The smaller the base image, the less likely that it includes unnecessary code, and hence the smaller the attack surface. Consider building from scratch (a completely empty image suitable for standalone binaries) or using a minimal base image such as distroless (*https://oreil.ly/kaUEc*). Smaller images also have the benefit of being quicker to send over the network.
> - Be thoughtful about using a tag or a digest to reference the base image. The build will be more reproducible if you use a digest, but it means you are less likely to pick up new versions of a base image that might include security updates. (That said, you should pick up missing updates through a vulnerability scan of your complete image.)

Use multi-stage builds
> The multi-stage build (*https://oreil.ly/k34z-*) is a way of eliminating unnecessary contents in the final image. An initial stage can include all the packages and toolchain required to build an image, but a lot of these tools are not needed at runtime. As an example, if you write an executable in Go, it needs the Go compiler in order to create an executable program. The container that runs the program doesn't need to have access to the Go compiler. In this example, it would be a good idea to break the build into a multi-stage build: one stage does the compilation and creates a binary executable; the next stage just has access to the standalone executable. The image that gets deployed has a much smaller attack surface;

a nonsecurity benefit is that the image itself will also be smaller, so the time to pull the image is reduced.

 Capital One has several multi-stage build examples (*https://oreil.ly/ CRMuY*) for node applications on its blog, showing how you can even run tests as different steps within a multi-stage build without impacting the contents of the final image.

Non-root USER

The USER instruction in a Dockerfile specifies that the default user identity for running containers based on this image isn't root. If you don't want all your containers running as root, specify a non-root user in all your Dockerfiles.

RUN commands

Let's be absolutely clear—a Dockerfile RUN command lets you run any arbitrary command. If an attacker can compromise the Dockerfile with the default security settings, that attacker can run *any code of their choosing*. If you have any reason not to trust people who can run arbitrary container builds on your system, I can't think of a better way of saying this: you have given them privileges for remote code execution. Make sure that privileges to edit Dockerfiles are limited to trusted members of your team, and pay close attention to code reviewing these changes. You might even want to institute a check or an audit log when any new or modified RUN commands are introduced in your Dockerfiles.

Volume mounts

Particularly for demos or tests, we often mount host directories into a container through volume mounts. As you will see in Chapter 9, it's important to check that Dockerfiles don't mount sensitive directories like /etc or /bin into a container.

Don't include sensitive data in the Dockerfile

We'll discuss sensitive data and secrets in more detail in Chapter 12, but for now please understand that including credentials, passwords, or other secret data in an image makes it easier for those secrets to be exposed.

Avoid setuid binaries

As discussed in Chapter 2, it's a good idea to avoid including executable files with the *setuid* bit, as these could potentially lead to privilege escalation.

Avoid unnecessary code

The smaller the amount of code in a container, the smaller the attack surface. Avoid adding packages, libraries, and executables into an image unless they are absolutely necessary. For the same reason, if you can base your image on the scratch image or one of the distroless options, you're likely to have dramatically less code—and hence less vulnerable code—in your image.

Include everything that your container needs

If the previous point exhorted you to exclude superfluous code from a build, this point is a corollary: *do* include everything that your application needs to operate. If you allow for the possibility of a container installing additional packages at runtime, how will you check that those packages are legitimate? It's far better to do all the installation and validation when the container image is built and create an immutable image. See "Immutable Containers" on page 87 for more on why this is a good idea.

Following these recommendations will help you build images that are harder to exploit. Now let's turn to the risk that an attacker will attempt to find weaknesses in your container build system.

Attacks on the Build Machine

The machine that builds the image is a concern for two main reasons:

- If an attacker can breach the build machine and run code on it, can they reach other parts of your system? As you saw in "The Dangers of docker build" on page 68, there are reasons to explore using a build tool that doesn't require a privileged daemon process.

- Can an attacker influence the outcome of a build so that you end up building, and ultimately running, malicious images? Any unauthorized access that interferes with a Dockerfile's instructions or that triggers unexpected builds can have disastrous consequences. For example, if an attacker can influence the code that's built, they could insert a backdoor into containers that run on your production deployment.

Given that your build machines create the code that you will ultimately run in your production cluster, it's critical to harden them against attack as if they were as important as the production cluster itself. Reduce the attack surface by eliminating unnecessary tools from build machines. Restrict direct user access to the machines, and protect them from unauthorized network access using VPCs and firewalls.

It is a good idea to run builds on a separate machine or cluster of machines from the production environment to limit the possible effects of a host attack from within a build. Limit network and cloud service access from this host to prevent an attacker from accessing other elements of your deployment.

Image Storage Security

Once the image is built it needs to be stored in a registry. If an attacker can replace or modify an image, this results in you running code of their choosing.

Running Your Own Registry

Many organizations maintain their own registries or use managed registries from their cloud provider and require that only images from those permitted registries can be used. Running your own registry (or your own instance of a managed registry) gives you more control and visibility over who can push and pull images. It also reduces the possibility of a DNS attack that allows an attacker to spoof the registry address. If the registry lives within a Virtual Private Cloud (VPC), it is highly unlikely that an attacker can do this.

Care should be taken to restrict direct access to the registry's storage media. For example, a registry running in AWS might use S3 to store images, and the S3 bucket(s) should have restrictive permissions so that a bad actor can't directly access stored image data.

Signing Images

Image signing associates an identity with an image (in much the same way as certificates are signed, which is covered in Chapter 11).

Image signing is quite complex, so it's unlikely that this is something you want to build for yourself. Various registries implement image signing based on the Notary implementation of the TUF (The Update Framework) specification (*https://oreil.ly/fMD6d*). Notary has a reputation for being difficult to use, so it's exciting that as I write, most if not all of the major cloud providers are getting involved with version 2 of this project.

Another project that addresses concerns about the supply chain for container images is in-toto (*https://in-toto.io/*). This framework ensures that each of an expected set of build steps ran completely, produced the correct output given the correct input, and was performed in the right order by the right people. Multiple steps are chained together, with in-toto carrying security-related metadata from each step through the process. The result is to ensure that software in production is verifiably running the same code as the developer shipped from their laptop.

What if you want to use a container image from a third party, either directly as an application or as a base image in your builds? You can take a signed image directly from the software vendor or from another trusted source, perhaps testing the image yourself before storing it in your own registry.

Image Deployment Security

The main security concern at deployment time is ensuring that the correct image gets pulled and run, although there are additional checks you might want to make through what is called *admission control*.

Deploying the Right Image

As you saw in "Identifying Images" on page 72, container image tags are not immutable—they can be moved to different versions of the same image. Referring to an image by its digest, rather than by tag, can help ensure that the image is the version that you think it is. However, if your build system tags images with semantic versioning and this is strictly adhered to, this may be sufficient and easier to manage since you don't necessarily have to update the image reference for every minor update.

If you refer to images by tag, you should always pull the latest version before running in case there has been an update. Fortunately, this is relatively efficient since the image manifest is retrieved first, and image layers have to be retrieved only if they have changed.

In Kubernetes, this is defined by the `imagePullPolicy`. An image policy to pull every time is unnecessary if you refer to images by digest, since any update would mean you have to change the digest.

Depending on your risk profile, you may also want to check the provenance of the image by checking for an image signature managed by a tool like the aforementioned Notary.

Malicious Deployment Definition

When you are using a container orchestrator, there typically are configuration files—YAML for Kubernetes, for instance—that define the containers that make up each application. It's just as important to verify the provenance of these configuration files as it is to check the images themselves.

If you download YAML from the internet, please check it *very* carefully before running it in your production cluster. Be aware that any small variations—such as the replacement of a single character in a registry URL—could result in a malicious image running on your deployment.

Admission Control

This is another topic that strays beyond the scope of pure container security, but I want to introduce the idea of admission control here because it's a good place to validate many of the ideas discussed earlier in this chapter.

An admission controller can perform checks at the point where you are about to deploy a resource into a cluster. In Kubernetes, admission control can evaluate any kind of resource against policies, but for the purposes of this chapter, I will just consider an admission controller that is checking whether to permit a container based on a particular container image. If the admission control checks fail, the container does not get run.

Admission controllers can perform several vital security checks on the container image before it is instantiated into a running container:

- Has the image been scanned for vulnerabilities/malware/other policy checks?
- Does the image come from a trusted registry?
- Is the image signed?
- Is the image approved?
- Does the image run as root?

These checks ensure that no one can bypass checks earlier in the system. For example, there is little advantage in introducing vulnerability scanning into your CI pipeline if it turns out that people can specify deployment instructions that refer to images that haven't been scanned.

GitOps and Deployment Security

GitOps is a methodology in which all the configuration information about the state of a system is held under source control, just as the application source code is. When a user wants to make an operational change to the system, they don't apply commands directly but instead check in the desired state in code form (for example, in YAML files for Kubernetes). An automated system called the GitOps operator makes sure that the system is updated to reflect the latest state as defined under code control.

This impacts security in significantly beneficial ways. Users no longer need direct access to the running system because everything is done at arm's length via the source code control system (typically Git, as the name implies). As shown in Figure 6-3, user credentials allow access to the source control system, but only the automated GitOps operator has permissions for modifying the running system. Because Git records every change, there is an audit trail for every operation.

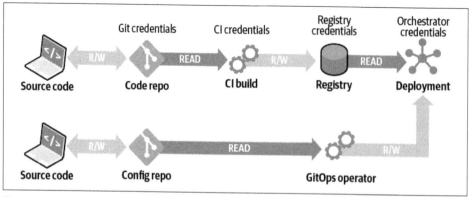

Figure 6-3. GitOps

Summary

You have seen how the container runtime needs a root filesystem and some configuration information. You can override the config using parameters that can be passed in at runtime or configured in Kubernetes YAML. Some of these configuration settings have a bearing on application security. There also will be plenty of opportunities to introduce malicious code into container images if you don't follow the best practices listed in "Dockerfile Best Practices for Security" on page 75.

The standard container image builders in common use at the time of writing tend to be privileged and present a number of weak points that you need to harden against attack, but there are alternative and more secure image builders available and in development.

At the point where images are deployed, orchestrators and security tools allow for admission controllers, which present an opportunity to perform security checks on those images.

Container images encapsulate your application code and any dependencies on third-party packages and libraries. The next chapter looks at how these dependencies could include exploitable vulnerabilities and examines tooling to identify and eliminate those vulnerabilities.

CHAPTER 7

Software Vulnerabilities in Images

Patching software for vulnerabilities has long been an important aspect of maintaining the security of deployed code. This is still a relevant problem in the world of containers, but as you will see in this chapter, the patching process has been completely reinvented. But first, let's cover what software vulnerabilities are and how they are published and tracked.

Vulnerability Research

A vulnerability is a known flaw in a piece of software that an attacker can take advantage of to perform some kind of malicious activity. As a general rule, you can assume that the more complex a piece of software is, the more likely it is to have flaws, some of which will be exploitable.

When there is a vulnerability in a common piece of software, attackers may be able to take advantage of it wherever it is deployed, so there is an entire research industry devoted to finding and reporting new vulnerabilities in publicly available software, especially operating system packages and language libraries. You have probably heard of some of the most devastating vulnerabilities, like Shellshock, Meltdown, and Heartbleed, which get not just a name but sometimes even a logo. These are the rock stars of the vulnerability world, but they are a tiny fraction of the thousands of issues that get reported every year.

Once a vulnerability is identified, the race is on to get a fix published so that users can deploy that fix before attackers take advantage of the issue. If new issues were announced to the public straightaway, this would create a free-for-all for attackers to take advantage of the problem. To avoid this, the concept of responsible security disclosures has been established. The security researcher who finds a vulnerability contacts the developer or vendor of the software in question. Both parties agree on a timeframe after which the researcher can publish their findings. There is some positive pressure here for the vendor to make efforts to provide a fix in a timely fashion, as it's better for both the vendor and its users that a fix is available before publication.

A new issue will get a unique identifier that begins with "CVE," which stands for Common Vulnerabilities and Exposures, followed by the year. For example, the Shell-Shock vulnerability was discovered in 2014 and is officially referred to as CVE-2014-6271. The organization that administers these IDs is called MITRE (*https://mitre.org*), and it oversees a number of CVE Numbering Authorities (CNAs) that can issue CVE IDs within certain scopes. Some large software vendors—for example, Microsoft, Red Hat, and Oracle—are CNAs entitled to assign IDs for vulnerabilities within their own products. GitHub became a CNA toward the end of 2019.

These CVE identifiers are used in the National Vulnerability Database (*https://nvd.nist.gov*) (NVD) to keep track of the software package and versions that are affected by each vulnerability. At first glance, you might be tempted to think that's the end of the story—there's a list of all the package versions that are affected, so if you have one of those versions, you are exposed. Unfortunately, it's not as simple as that, because depending on the Linux distribution you're using, it might have a patched version of the package.

Vulnerabilities, Patches, and Distributions

Let's take a look at ShellShock as an example. This was a critical vulnerability that affected the GNU bash package, and the NVD's page for CVE-2014-6271 (*https://oreil.ly/XGgEb*) has a long list of vulnerable versions ranging from 1.14.0 to 4.3. If you're running a very old installation of Ubuntu 12.04 and you found that your server has bash version 4.2-2ubuntu2.2, you might think that it is vulnerable because it's based on bash 4.2, which is included in the NVD's list for ShellShock.

In fact, according to the Ubuntu security advisory for the same vulnerability (*https://oreil.ly/IEUqF*), that exact version has the fix for the vulnerability applied, so it's safe. The Ubuntu maintainers decided that rather than require everyone on 12.04 to upgrade to a whole new minor version of bash, they would apply the patch for the vulnerability and make that patched version available.

To get a real picture of whether the packages installed on a server are vulnerable or not, you would need to reference not just the NVD but also the security advisories that apply to your distribution.

So far this chapter has considered packages (like bash in the preceding example) that are distributed in binary form through package managers such as apt, yum, rpm, or apk. These packages are shared across all the applications in a filesystem, and on a server or virtual machine the fact that they are shared can cause no end of problems:

one application may depend on a certain version of a package that turns out to be incompatible with another application that you want to run on the same machine. This issue of dependency management is one of the problems that containers can address by having a separate root filesystem for each container.

Application-Level Vulnerabilities

There are also vulnerabilities to be found at the application level. Most applications use third-party libraries that are typically installed using a language-specific package manager. Node.js uses npm, Python uses pip, Java uses Maven, and so on. The third-party packages installed by these tools are another source of potential vulnerabilities.

In compiled languages like Go, C, and Rust, your third-party dependencies could be installed as shared libraries, or they could be linked into your binary at build time.

A standalone binary executable by definition (through the word "standalone") has no external dependencies. It may have dependencies on third-party libraries or packages, but these are built into the executable. In this case you have the option of creating a container image based on the scratch (empty) base image, which holds nothing but your binary executable.

If an application doesn't have any dependencies, it can't be scanned for published package vulnerabilities. It could still have flaws that render it exploitable by attackers, which we will consider in "Zero-Day Vulnerabilities" on page 94.

Vulnerability Risk Management

Dealing with software vulnerabilities is an important aspect of risk management. It's very likely that a deployment of any nontrivial software will include some vulnerabilities, and there is a risk that systems will be attacked through them. To manage this risk, you need to be able to identify which vulnerabilities are present and assess their severity, prioritize them, and have processes in place to fix or mitigate these issues.

Vulnerability scanners automate the process of identifying vulnerabilities. They provide information about how serious each issue is and about the software package version in which a fix was applied (if a fix has been made available).

Vulnerability Scanning

If you search the internet, you will find a huge range of vulnerability scanning tools encompassing various techniques, including port scanning tools like nmap and nessus that attempt to find vulnerabilities on a live running system by probing it from outside. This is a valuable approach, but it's not what we are considering in this chapter.

Here, we are more interested in tools that help you find vulnerabilities by examining the software that is installed in a root filesystem.

To identify which vulnerabilities are present, the first task is to establish what software is present. Software gets installed through several different mechanisms:

- The root filesystem starts from a distribution of a Linux root filesystem, which could have vulnerabilities within it.

- There could be system packages installed by a Linux package manager like rpm or apk, and language-specific packages installed by tools like pip or RubyGems.

- You might have installed some software directly using wget, curl, or even FTP.

Some vulnerability scanners will query package managers to get a list of the installed software. If you're using one of those tools, you should avoid installing software directly as it won't be scanned for vulnerabilities.

Installed Packages

As you have seen in Chapter 6, each container image could include a Linux distribution, possibly with some packages installed, along with its application code. There could be many running instances of each container, each of which has its own copy of the container image filesystem, including any vulnerable packages that might be included therein. This is illustrated in Figure 7-1, where there are two instances of container X and one instance of container Y. In addition, the illustration shows some packages installed directly onto the host machine.

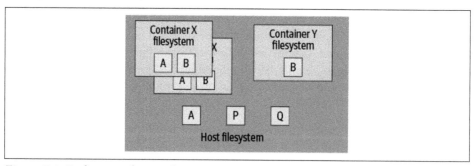

Figure 7-1. Packages on host and in containers

Installing packages directly onto hosts is nothing new—in fact, it is exactly these packages that system administrators have traditionally had to patch for security reasons. This was often achieved by simply SSH-ing into each host and installing the patched package. In the cloud native era, this is frowned upon, because manually modifying the state of a machine in this way means that it can't be automatically re-created in the same state. Instead, it's better either to build a new machine image with the updated packages or to update the automation scripts used to provision images so that new installations include the updated packages.

Container Image Scanning

To know whether your deployment is running containers with vulnerable software, you need to scan all the dependencies within those containers. There are some different approaches you could take to achieve this.

Imagine a tool that can scan each running container on a host (or across a deployment of multiple hosts). In today's cloud native deployments, it's common to see hundreds of instances of containers initiated from the same container image, so a scanner that takes this approach would be very inefficient, looking at the same dependencies hundreds of times. It's far more efficient to scan the container image from which these containers were derived.

However, this approach relies on the containers running only the software that was present in the container image and nothing else. The code running in each container must be *immutable*. Let's see why it's a good idea to treat containers as immutable in this way.

Immutable Containers

There is (usually) nothing to stop a container from downloading additional software into its filesystem after it starts running. Indeed, in the early days of containers, it was not uncommon to see this pattern, as it was considered a way to update the container to the latest version of software without having to rebuild the container image. If this idea hadn't occurred to you before now, please try to wipe it from your memory straightaway, as it's generally considered a very bad idea for several reasons, including these:

- If your container downloads code at runtime, different instances of the container could be running different versions of that code, but it would be difficult to know which instance is running what version. Without a stored version of that container's code, it can be hard (or even impossible) to re-create an identical copy. This is a problem when trying to reproduce field issues.

- It's harder to control and ensure the provenance of the software running in each container if it could be downloaded at any time and from anywhere.

- Building a container image and storing it in a registry is very simple to automate in a CI/CD pipeline. It's also very easy to add additional security checks—like vulnerability scanning or verification of the software supply chain—into the same pipeline.

A lot of production deployments treat containers as immutable simply as a best practice, but without enforcement. There are tools that can automatically enforce container immutability by preventing an executable from running in a container if that executable wasn't present in the image when it was scanned. This is known as *drift prevention* and is discussed further in Chapter 13.

Another way to achieve immutability is to run the container with a read-only filesystem. You can mount a writable temporary filesystem if the application code needs access to writable local storage. This may require changes to the application so that it writes only to this temporary filesystem.

By treating your containers as immutable, you only need to scan each image to find all the vulnerabilities that might be present in all the containers. But unfortunately, scanning just once at a single point in time may not be sufficient. Let's consider why scans have to happen on a regular basis.

Regular Scanning

As discussed at the beginning of this chapter, there is a body of security researchers around the world who are finding previously undiscovered vulnerabilities in existing code. Sometimes they find issues that have been present for years. One of the best-known examples of this is HeartBleed, a critical vulnerability in the widely used OpenSSL package that exploited a problem in the heartbeat request and response flow that keeps a TLS connection alive. The vulnerability was uncovered in April 2014, and it allowed an attacker to send a crafted heartbeat request that asked for a small amount of data in a large buffer. The absence of a length check in the OpenSSL code meant that the response would supply the small amount of data, followed by whatever happened to be in active memory to fill up the rest of the response buffer. That memory might be holding sensitive data, which would be returned to the attacker. Serious data breaches that involved the loss of passwords, Social Security numbers, and medical records were subsequently traced back to the Heartbleed vulnerability.

Cases as serious as HeartBleed are rare, but it makes sense to assume that if you're using a third-party dependency, at some point in the future a new vulnerability will be uncovered in it. And unfortunately there is no way of knowing when that will happen. Even if your code doesn't change, there is a possibility that new vulnerabilities have been uncovered within its dependencies.

Regularly rescanning container images allows the scanning tool to check the contents against its most up-to-date knowledge about vulnerabilities (from the NVD and other security advisory sources). A very common approach is to rescan all deployed images every 24 hours, in addition to scanning new images as they are built, as part of an automated CI/CD pipeline.

Scanning Tools

There are numerous container image scanning tools, from open source implementations like Trivy (*https://oreil.ly/SxKQT*), Clair (*https://oreil.ly/avK-2*), and Anchore (*https://oreil.ly/7rFFt*) to commercial solutions from companies like JFrog, Palo Alto, and Aqua. Many container image registry solutions, such as Docker Trusted Registry (*https://docs.docker.com/ee/dtr*) and the CNCF project Harbor (*https://goharbor.io*), as well as the registries provided by the major public clouds, include scanning as a built-in feature.

Unfortunately, the results you get from different scanners vary considerably, and it's worth considering why.

Sources of Information

As discussed earlier in this chapter, there are various sources for vulnerability information, including per-distribution security advisories. Red Hat even has more than one (*https://oreil.ly/jE4ad*)—its OVAL feed includes only vulnerabilities for which there is a fix, not those that have been published but are not yet fixed.

If a scanner doesn't include data from a distribution's security feed and is relying just on the underlying NVD data, it is likely to show a lot of false positives for images based on that distribution. If you prefer a particular Linux distribution for your base images, or a solution like distroless, make sure that your image scanner supports it.

Out-of-Date Sources

Occasionally the distribution maintainers change the way they are reporting vulnerabilities. This happened fairly recently with Alpine, which stopped updating its advisories at alpine-secdb (*https://oreil.ly/lVHll*) in favor of a new system at aports (*https://oreil.ly/J1-YA*). As of this writing, some scanners are still only reporting data from the old Alpine feed, which hasn't been updated in several months.

Won't Fix Vulnerabilities

Sometimes the maintainers of a distribution will decide that they are not going to fix a particular vulnerability (perhaps because it's a negligible risk and the fix is nontrivial, or because the maintainers have concluded that interactions with other packages on their platform mean the vulnerability is impossible to exploit).

Given that the maintainers are not going to provide a fix, it becomes something of a philosophical question for scanner tool developers: considering it's not actionable, do you show the vulnerability in the results or not? At Aqua we heard from some of our customers that they don't want to see this category of result, so we provide an option to give the user the choice. It just goes to show that there is no such thing as a "correct" set of results when it comes to vulnerability scanning.

Subpackage Vulnerabilities

Sometimes a package is installed and reported by the package manager, but in fact it consists of one or more subpackages. A good example of this is the bind package on Ubuntu. Sometimes this is installed with only the docs subpackage, which, as you might imagine, consists only of documentation. Some scanners assume that if the package is reported, then the whole package (including all its possible subpackages) is installed. This can result in false positives where the scanner reports vulnerabilities that can't be present because the guilty subpackage is not installed.

Package Name Differences

The source name for a package may include binaries that have completely different names. For example, in Debian, the shadow (*https://oreil.ly/SpPXQ*) package includes binaries called login, passwd, and uidmap. If the scanner doesn't take this into account, it can result in false negative results.

Additional Scanning Features

A few image scanners detect other issues in addition to vulnerabilities, such as:

- Known malware within the image
- Executables with the *setuid* bit (which, as you saw in Chapter 2, can allow privilege escalation)
- Images configured to run as root
- Secret credentials such as tokens or passwords
- Sensitive data in the form of credit card or Social Security numbers or something similar

Scanner Errors

As I hope this section of the book has made clear, reporting on vulnerabilities is not as straightforward as you might at first imagine. So it's very likely that in any scanner you will find cases in which there is a false positive or false negative due to a bug in the scanner or a flaw in the security advisory data feeds that the scanner reads.

That said, it's better to have a scanner in place than not. If you don't have a scanner in place and use it regularly, you really have no way of knowing whether your software is prey to an easy exploit. Time is no healer in this regard—the critical Shellshock vulnerability was discovered in code that was decades old. If you rely on complex dependencies, you should expect that at some point some vulnerabilities will be found within them.

False positives can be irritating, but some tools will let you whitelist individual vulnerability reports so that you can decide for yourself whether you want to accept them going forward.

Assuming that you are convinced that a scanner would be a good thing to include in your processes, let's turn to the possible options for incorporating it into your team's workflow.

Scanning in the CI/CD Pipeline

Consider a CI/CD pipeline from left to right, with "writing code" at the far left and "deploying to production" at the far right, as in Figure 7-2. It's better to remove issues as early as possible in this pipeline because doing so is quicker and cheaper, in exactly the same way that finding and fixing bugs is much more time-consuming and expensive after deployment than during development.

In a traditional host-based deployment, all the software running on a host shares the same packages. The security team in an organization would typically be responsible for updating those packages with security fixes on a regular basis. This activity is largely decoupled from the development and testing stages of each application's life cycle, and it's way over to the right in the deployment pipeline. There often can be issues where different applications share the same package but need different versions, requiring careful dependency management and, in some cases, code changes.

In contrast, as you saw in Chapter 6, in a container-based deployment each image includes its own dependencies, so different application containers can have their own versions of each package as needed. There is no need to worry about compatibility between app code and the set of dependencies they use. This, plus the existence of container image scanning tools, allows vulnerability management to "shift left" in the pipeline.

Teams can include vulnerability scanning as an automated step. When a vulnerability needs to be addressed, developers can do this by updating and rebuilding their application container image to include the patched version. Security teams no longer need to do this manually.

There are a few places where scanning can be introduced, as illustrated in Figure 7-2.

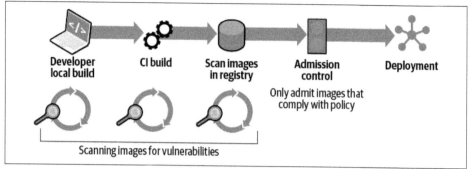

Figure 7-2. Scanning for vulnerabilities in the CI/CD pipeline

Developer scanning

If you use a scanner that is easy to deploy on the desktop, individual developers can scan their local image builds for issues, giving them the chance to fix them before they push to a source code repository.

Scan on build

Consider incorporating a scanning step immediately after the container image is built in your pipeline. If the scan reveals vulnerabilities above a certain severity level, you can fail the build to ensure that it never gets deployed. Figure 7-3 shows the output from an AWS CodeBuild project that builds an image from a Dockerfile and then scans it. In this example, a high-severity vulnerability was detected, and this has caused the build to fail.

Figure 7-3. Example of failing a build when a high-severity vulnerability is detected

Registry scans

After the image has been built, the pipeline typically pushes it to an image registry. It's a good idea to regularly scan images in case a new vulnerability has been found in a package that's used by an image that hasn't been rebuilt in a while.

 The following articles have useful details on how to incorporate various scanners within different CI/CD pipeline solutions:

- "Scanning images with Trivy in an AWS CodePipeline" (*https://oreil.ly/6ANm9*)
- "Container Scanning" on GitLab (*https://oreil.ly/okLcm*)
- "Docker Image Scanning in your Codefresh Pipeline with Aqua" (*https://oreil.ly/P5_59*)

You probably don't want to leave the scan step until the point of deployment, for the simple reason that you would scan every instance of the container as it gets instantiated, even though these instances all come from the same container image. Assuming that you can treat the container as immutable, it's the image and not the container that you should scan.

Prevent Vulnerable Images from Running

It's one thing to use a scanner to establish whether an image has any significant vulnerabilities, but you also need to make sure that vulnerable images don't get deployed. This can be done as part of the admission control step that we considered in "Admission Control" on page 79, as indicated in Figure 7-2. If there isn't a check to ensure that only scanned images can be deployed, it would be relatively easy to bypass the vulnerability scanner.

Generally speaking, commercial vulnerability scanners are sold as part of a broader platform that also correlates admission control with scan results. In a Kubernetes deployment, you can use Open Policy Agent to enforce custom admission control checks, which could include checking that images have passed their vulnerability scan. Google is also working on this capability as part of the Kritis (*https://oreil.ly/PIhQu*) project.

So far in this chapter we have discussed known vulnerabilities in dependencies that your application code relies on. But this misses out on an important category of vulnerabilities called *zero days*.

Zero-Day Vulnerabilities

"Vulnerability Research" on page 83 discussed how there are security researchers around the world looking for new ways to exploit existing software. It stands to reason that when a new vulnerability is found, some amount of time passes before a fix is published that addresses the problem. Until a fix is made available, the vulnerability is known as a *zero-day* or *0-day* vulnerability because no days have passed since the fix was published. (It is not so long since it was considered acceptable to wait for up to, say, thirty days before applying a security patch. The mind boggles at how many attacks could be attempted in this length of time.)

If it's possible for a third-party library to have a bug that an attacker can exploit, the same is true for any code—including the applications that your team is writing. Peer review, static analysis, and testing can all help to identify security issues in your code, but there's a chance that some issues will slip through. Depending on your organization and the value of its data, there may be bad actors in the world for whom it's worthwhile trying to find these flaws.

The good news is that if a vulnerability isn't published, the vast majority of potential attackers in the world don't know about it, any more than you do.

The bad news is that you can bet on the fact that sophisticated attackers and nation-state organizations have libraries of as-yet-unpublished vulnerabilities. We know this to be true from Edward Snowden's revelations (*https://oreil.ly/Yz1tJ*).

No amount of matching against a vulnerability database is going to be able to identify a vulnerability that hasn't been published yet. Depending on the type and severity of the exploit, sandboxing as described in Chapter 8 may well protect your application and your data. Your best hope for defending against zero-day exploits is to detect and prevent anomalous behavior at runtime, which I will discuss in Chapter 13.

Summary

In this chapter, you read about vulnerability research and the CVE identifiers that are assigned to different vulnerability issues. You saw why it's important to have distributions-specific security advisory information and to not just rely on the NVD. You know why different scanners can produce different results, so you are better armed to make a decision about which tools to use. Whichever scanner you pick, I hope you're now convinced that you need container image scanning built into your CI/CD pipeline.

CHAPTER 8

Strengthening Container Isolation

Back in Chapters 3 and 4, you saw how containers create some separation between workloads even though they are running on the same host. In this chapter, you'll learn about some more advanced tools and techniques that can be used to strengthen the isolation between workloads.

Suppose you have two workloads and you don't want them to be able to interfere with each other. One approach is to isolate them so that they are unaware of each other, which at a high level is really what containers and virtual machines are doing. Another approach is to limit the actions those workloads can take so that even if one workload is somehow aware of the other, it is unable to take actions to affect that workload. Isolating an application so that it has limited access to resources is known as *sandboxing*.

When you run an application as a container, the container acts as a convenient object for sandboxing. Every time you start a container, you know what application code is supposed to be running inside that container. If the application were to be compromised, the attacker might try to run code that is outside that application's normal behavior. By using sandboxing mechanisms, we can limit what that code can do, restricting the attacker's ability to affect the system. The first mechanism we'll consider is *seccomp*.

Seccomp

In "System Calls" on page 13, you saw that system calls provide the interface for an application to ask the kernel to perform certain operations on the application's behalf. Seccomp is a mechanism for restricting the set of system calls that an application is allowed to make.

When it was first introduced to the Linux kernel back in 2005, seccomp (for "secure computing mode") meant that a process, once it had transitioned to this mode, could make only a very few system calls:

- `sigreturn` (return from a signal handler)
- `exit` (terminate the process)
- `read` and `write`, but only using file descriptors that were already open before the transition to secure mode

Untrusted code could be run in this mode without being able to achieve anything malicious. Unfortunately, the side effect is that lots of code couldn't really achieve anything at all useful in this mode. The sandbox was simply too limited.

In 2012, a new approach called *seccomp-bpf* was added to the kernel. This uses Berkeley Packet Filters to determine whether or not a given system call is permitted, based on a seccomp profile applied to the process. Each process can have its own profile.

The BPF seccomp filter can look at the system call opcode and the parameters to the call to make a decision about whether the call is permitted by the profile. In fact, it's slightly more complicated than that: the profile indicates what to do when a syscall matches a given filter, with possible actions including return an error, terminate the process, or call a tracer. But for most uses in the world of containers, the profile either permits a system call or returns an error, so you can think of it as whitelisting or blacklisting a set of system calls.

This can be very useful in the container world because there are several system calls that a containerized application really has no business trying to make, except under extremely unusual circumstances. For example, you really don't want any of your containerized apps to be able to change the clock time on the host machine, so it makes sense to block access to the syscalls `clock_adjtime` and `clock_settime`. It's unlikely that you want containers to be making changes to kernel modules, so there is no need for them to call `create_module`, `delete_module`, or `init_module`. There is a keyring in the Linux kernel, and it isn't namespaced, so it's a good idea to block containers from making calls to `request_key` or `keyctl`.

The Docker default seccomp profile (*https://oreil.ly/3sNNI*) blocks more than 40 of the 300+ syscalls (including all the examples just listed) without ill effects on the vast majority of containerized applications. Unless you have a reason not to do so, it's a good default profile to use.

Unfortunately, although it's used by default in Docker, there is no seccomp profile applied by default using Kubernetes (even if you're using Docker as the container runtime). At least at the time of writing, support for seccomp is an Alpha feature, and you can apply profiles using annotations on PodSecurityPolicy (*https://oreil.ly/6gIjt*) objects.

> Jess Frazelle uses a seccomp profile to great effect on contained.af to demonstrate the strength of containers+seccomp isolation—it hasn't been breached as of this writing, despite attempts over several years.

You might want to go even further and limit a container to an even smaller group of syscalls—in an ideal world, there would be a tailored profile for each application that permits precisely the set of syscalls that it needs. There are a few different possible approaches to creating this kind of profile:

- You can use `strace` to trace out all the system calls being called by your application. Jess Frazelle describes how she did this to generate and test the default Docker seccomp profile in this blog post (*https://oreil.ly/ROlHh*).

- A more modern way to get the list of systems calls is with an eBPF-based utility. Bearing in mind that seccomp uses BPF to limit the set of syscalls that are permitted, it's no great surprise that you can use eBPF (for "extended Berkeley Packet Filter") to get the list of syscalls that it uses. You can use tools like falco2seccomp (*https://oreil.ly/z5yyT*) or Tracee (*https://oreil.ly/iw-rL*) to list the system calls being generated by a container.

- If creating seccomp profiles yourself seems like a lot of effort, you may wish to look at commercial container security tools, some of which have the ability to observe individual workloads in order to automatically generate custom seccomp profiles.

> If you are interested in the underlying technology behind `strace`, you might like to watch this talk (*https://oreil.ly/SV6d-*) in which I create a very basic `strace` implementation in a few lines of Go.

AppArmor

AppArmor (*https://gitlab.com/apparmor*) (short for "Application Armor") is one of a handful of Linux security modules (LSM) that can be enabled in the Linux kernel. In AppArmor, a profile can be associated with an executable file, determining what that file is allowed to do in terms of capabilities and file access permissions. You'll recall that these were both covered in Chapter 2. To see whether AppArmor is enabled in your kernel, look in the file */sys/module/apparmor/parameters/enabled*—if you find y, then AppArmor is enabled.

AppArmor and other LSMs implement *mandatory access controls*. A mandatory access control is set by a central administrator, and once set, other users do not have any ability to modify the control or pass it on to another user. This is in contrast to Linux file permissions, which are *discretionary access controls*, in the sense that if my user account owns a file, I could grant your user access to it (unless this is overridden by a mandatory access control), or I could set it as unwritable even by my own user account to prevent myself from inadvertently changing it. Using mandatory access controls gives the administrator much more granular control of what can happen on their system, in a way that individual users can't override.

AppArmor includes a "complain" mode in which you can run your executable against a profile and any violations get logged. The idea is that you can use these logs to update the profile, with the goal of eventually seeing no new violations, at which point you start to enforce the profile.

 To create AppArmor profiles for containers, you should consider using bane (*https://oreil.ly/Xe7YZ*).

Once you have a profile, you install it under the /etc/apparmor directory and run a tool called apparmor_parser to load it. See which profiles are loaded by looking at /sys/kernel/security/apparmor/profiles.

Running a container using docker run --security-opt="apparmor:<profile name>" ... will constrain the container to the behaviors permitted by the profile. Containerd and CRI-O also support AppArmor.

There is a default Docker AppArmor profile, but be aware that, as with the seccomp one, Kubernetes does not use it by default. You will need to add annotations (*https://oreil.ly/_ll08*) to use any AppArmor profile on a container in a Kubernetes pod.

SELinux

SELinux, or "Security-Enhanced Linux," is another type of LSM, this time developed by Red Hat, although history (or at least Wikipedia (*https://oreil.ly/gV7_e*)) relates that it has its roots in projects by the US National Security Agency. If you're running a Red Hat distribution (RHEL or Centos) on your hosts, there is a good chance that SELinux is enabled already.

SELinux lets you constrain what a process is allowed to do in terms of its interactions with files and other processes. Each process runs under an SELinux *domain*—you can think of this as the context that the process is running in—and every file has a type. You can inspect the SELinux information associated with each file by running `ls -lZ`, and similarly you can add `-Z` to the `ps` command to get the SELinux detail for processes.

A key distinction between SELinux permissions and regular DAC Linux permissions (as seen in Chapter 2) is that in SELinux, permissions have nothing to do with the user identity—they are described entirely by labels. That said, they work together, so an action has to be permitted by both DAC and SELinux.

Every file on the machine has to be labeled with its SELinux information before you can enforce policies. These policies can dictate what access a process of a particular domain has to files of a particular type. In practical terms, this means that you can limit an application to have access only to its own files and prevent any other processes from being able to access those files. In the event that an application becomes compromised, this limits the set of files that it can affect, even if the normal discretionary access controls would have permitted it. When SELinux is enabled, it has a mode in which policy violations are logged rather than enforced (similar to what we saw in AppArmor).

Creating an effective SELinux profile for an application takes in-depth knowledge of the set of files that it might need access to, in both happy and error paths, so that task may be best left to the app developer. Some vendors provide profiles for their applications.

If you are interested in learning more about SELinux, there is a good tutorial on the subject by DigitalOcean (*https://oreil.ly/2Hx6b*), or you might prefer Dan Walsh's visual guide (*https://oreil.ly/jmhC-*). Project Atomic provides details on how SELinux interacts with Docker (*https://oreil.ly/msyOa*).

The security mechanisms we have seen so far—seccomp, AppArmor, and SELinux—all police a process's behavior at a low level. Generating a complete profile in terms of the precise set of systems calls or capabilities needed can be a difficult job, and a small change to an application can require a significant change to the profile in order to run. The administrative overhead of keeping profiles in line with applications as they change can be a burden, and human nature means there is a tendency either to use loose profiles or to turn them off altogether. The default Docker seccomp and AppArmor profiles provide some useful guardrails if you don't have the resources to generate per-application profiles.

It's worth noting, however, that although these protection mechanisms limit what the user space application can do, there is still a shared kernel. A vulnerability within the kernel itself, like Dirty COW (*https://oreil.ly/qQiJL*), would not be prevented by any of these tools.

So far in this chapter you have seen security mechanisms that can be applied to a container to limit what that container is permitted to do. Now let's turn to a set of sandboxing techniques that fall somewhere between container and virtual machine isolation, starting with gVisor.

gVisor

Google's gVisor sandboxes a container by intercepting system calls in much the same way that a hypervisor intercepts the system calls of a guest virtual machine.

According to the gVisor documentation (*https://gvisor.dev/docs*), gVisor is a "user-space kernel," which strikes me as a contradiction in terms but is meant to describe how a number of Linux system calls are implemented in user space through paravirtualization. As you saw in Chapter 5, paravirtualization means reimplementing instructions that would otherwise be run by the host kernel.

To do this, a component of gVisor called the Sentry intercepts syscalls from the application. Sentry is heavily sandboxed using seccomp, such that it is unable to access filesystem resources itself. When it needs to make system calls related to file access, it off-loads them to an entirely separate process called the Gofer.

Even those system calls that are unrelated to filesystem access are not passed through to the host kernel directly but instead are reimplemented within the Sentry. Essentially it's a guest kernel, operating in user space.

The gVisor project (*https://oreil.ly/cMROh*) provides an executable called runc that is compatible with OCI-format bundles and acts very much like the regular runc OCI runtime that we met in Chapter 6. Running a container with runsc allows you to easily see the gVisor processes, but if you have an existing config.json file for runc, you will probably need to regenerate a runsc-compatible version. In the following example I am running the same bundle for Alpine Linux that I used in "OCI Standards" on page 66:

```
$ cd alpine-bundle
# Store the existing config.json that works with runc
$ mv config.json config.json.runc
# Create a config.json file for runsc
$ runsc spec
$ sudo runsc run sh
```

In a second terminal you can use runsc list to see containers created by runsc:

```
$ runsc list
ID  PID     STATUS   BUNDLE                        CREATED              OWNER
sh  32258   running  /home/vagrant/alpine-bundle   2019-08-26T13:51:21  root
```

Inside the container, run a `sleep` command for long enough that you can observe it from the second terminal. The `runsc ps <container ID>` shows the processes running inside the container:

```
$ runsc ps sh
UID       PID       PPID      C         STIME     TIME      CMD
0         1         0         0         14:06     10ms      sh
0         15        1         0         14:15     0s        sleep
```

So far, so much as expected, but things get very interesting if you start to look at the processes from the host's perspective (the output here was edited to show the interesting parts):

```
$ ps fax
  PID TTY       STAT    TIME COMMAND
  ...
 3226 pts/1     S+      0:00 |        \_ sudo runsc run sh
 3227 pts/1     Sl+     0:00 |           \_ runsc run sh
 3231 pts/1     Sl+     0:00 |              \_ runsc-gofer --root=/var/run/runsc
 3234 ?         Ssl     0:00 |              \_ runsc-sandbox --root=/var/run/runsc
 3248 ?         tsl     0:00 |                 \_ [exe]
 3257 ?         tl      0:00 |                    \_ [exe]
 3266 ?         tl      0:00 |                    \_ [exe]
 3270 ?         tl      0:00 |                    \_ [exe]
  ...
```

You can see the `runsc run` process, which has spawned two processes: one is for the Gofer; the other is `runsc-sandbox` but is referred to as the Sentry in the gVisor documentation. Sandbox has a child process that in turn has three children of its own. Looking at the process information for these child and grandchild processes from the host's perspective reveals something interesting: all four of them are running the `runsc` executable. For brevity the following example shows the child and one grandchild:

```
$ ls -l /proc/3248/exe
lrwxrwxrwx 1 nobody nogroup 0 Aug 26 14:11 /proc/3248/exe -> /usr/local/bin/runsc
$ ls -l /proc/3257/exe
lrwxrwxrwx 1 nobody nogroup 0 Aug 26 14:13 /proc/3257/exe -> /usr/local/bin/runsc
```

Notably, none of these processes refers to the `sleep` executable that we know is running inside the container because we can see it with `runsc ps`. Trying to find that `sleep` executable more directly from the host is also unsuccessful:

```
vagrant@vagrant:~$ sudo ps -eaf | grep sleep
vagrant  3554 3171  0 14:26 pts/2    00:00:00 grep --color=auto sleep
```

This inability to see the processes running inside the gVisor sandbox is much more akin to the behavior you see in a regular VM than it is like a normal container. And it affords extra protection for the processes running inside the sandbox: even if an attacker gets root access on a host, there is still a relatively strong boundary between the host and the running processes. Or least there would be, were it not for the `runsc` command itself! It offers an `exec` subcommand that we can use, as root on the host, to operate inside a running container:

```
$ sudo runsc exec sh ps
PID   USER     TIME  COMMAND
   1 root      0:00 /bin/sh
  21 root      0:00 sleep 100
  22 root      0:00 ps
```

While this isolation looks very powerful, there are two significant limitations:

- The first is that not all Linux syscalls (*https://oreil.ly/PHsFm*) have been implemented in gVisor. If your application wants to use any of the unimplemented syscalls, it can't run inside gVisor. At the time of this writing, 97 systems were not available in gVisor. This compares to around 44 syscalls that are blocked by the default Docker seccomp profile (*https://oreil.ly/Lt5Ge*).

- The second is performance. In many cases performance is very close to that achieved with `runc`, but if your application makes a lot of system calls, its performance may well be impacted. The gVisor project published a performance guide (*https://oreil.ly/zqC6i*) to help you explore this in more detail.

Because gVisor reimplements the kernel, it's large and complex, and that complexity suggests a relatively high chance of including some vulnerabilities of its own (like this privilege escalation (*https://oreil.ly/awCYt*) discovered by Max Justicz).

As you have seen in this section, gVisor provides an isolation mechanism that more closely resembles a virtual machine than a regular container. However, gVisor affects only the way that an application accesses system calls. Namespaces, cgroups, and changing the root are still used to isolate the container.

The rest of this chapter discusses approaches that use virtual machine isolation for running containerized applications.

Kata Containers

As you've seen in Chapter 4, when you run a regular container, the container runtime starts a new process within the host. The idea with Kata Containers (*https://katacon tainers.io*) is to run containers within a separate virtual machine. This approach gives the ability to run applications from regular OCI format container images, with all the isolation of a virtual machine.

Kata uses a proxy between the container runtime and a separate target host where the application code runs. The runtime proxy creates a separate virtual machine using QEMU to run the container on its behalf.

One criticism of Kata Containers is that you have to wait for a virtual machine to boot up. The folks at AWS have created a lightweight virtual machine that is specifically designed for running containers, with much faster startup times than a normal VM: Firecracker.

Firecracker

As you saw in "Disadvantages of Virtual Machines" on page 62, virtual machines are slow to start, making them unsuitable for the ephemeral workloads that typically run in containers. But what if you had a virtual machine that boots extremely quickly? Firecracker (*https://oreil.ly/ZkPef*) is a virtual machine offering the benefits of secure isolation through a hypervisor and no shared kernel, but with startup times around 100ms, it is much more suitable for containers. It has the benefit of becoming field-hardened due to its (as I understand it, gradual) adoption by AWS for its Lambda and Fargate services.

Firecracker is able to start up so fast because its designers have stripped out functionality that is generally included in a kernel but that isn't required in a container. Enumerating devices is one of the slowest parts of booting a system, but containerized applications rarely have a reason to use many devices. The main saving comes from a minimal device model that strips out all but the essential devices.

Firecracker runs in user space, with a REST API for configuring guests to run under the Firecracker VMM. It uses KVM-based hardware virtualization for its guest operating systems, so you can't run it within, say, a Type 2–based guest OS on your laptop, unless your combination of hardware and software supports nested virtualization.

There is one last approach to isolation that I'd like to cover in this chapter, and it takes an even more extreme approach to reducing the size of the guest operating system: Unikernels.

Unikernels

The operating system that runs in a virtual machine image is a general-purpose offering that you can reuse for any application. It stands to reason that apps are unlikely to use every feature of the operating system. If you were able to drop the unused parts, there would be a smaller attack surface.

The idea of Unikernels is to create a dedicated machine image consisting of the application and the parts of the operating system that the app needs. This machine image can run directly on the hypervisor, giving the same levels of isolation as regular virtual machines, but with a lightweight startup time similar to what we see in Firecracker.

Every application has to be compiled into a Unikernel image complete with everything it needs to operate. The hypervisor can boot up this machine in just the same way that it would boot a standard Linux virtual machine image.

IBM's Nabla (*https://oreil.ly/W_BRY*) project makes use of Unikernel techniques for containers. Nabla containers use a highly restricted set of just seven system calls, with this policed by a seccomp profile. All other system calls from the application get handled within a Unikernel library OS component. By accessing only a small proportion of the kernel, Nabla containers reduce the attack surface. The downside is that you need to rebuild your applications in Nabla container form.

Summary

In this chapter, you have seen that there are a variety of ways to isolate instances of application code from one another, which look to some degree like what we understand as a "container":

- Some options use regular containers, with additional security mechanisms applied to bolster basic container isolation: seccomp, AppArmor, SELinux. These are proven and battle-tested but also renowned for how hard they are to manage effectively.
- There are new solutions that give the isolation of a virtual machine: Firecracker and Unikernels.
- Finally, there is a third category of sandboxing techniques such as gVisor that fall somewhere between container and virtual machine isolation.

What's right for your applications depends on your risk profile, and your decision may be influenced by the options offered by your public cloud and/or managed solution. Regardless of the container runtime you use and the isolation it enforces, there are ways that a user can easily compromise this isolation. Move on to Chapter 9 to see how.

Breaking Container Isolation

In Chapter 4, you saw how a container is constructed and how it gets a limited view of the machine it is running on. In this chapter, you'll see how easy it is to configure containers to run in such a way that this isolation is effectively broken.

Sometimes you will want to do this deliberately, to achieve something specific such as off-loading networking functionality to a sidecar container. In other circumstances, the ideas discussed in this chapter could be seriously compromising the security of your applications!

To start with, let's talk about what is arguably the most insecure-by-default behavior in the container world: running as root.

Containers Run as Root by Default

Unless your container image specifies a non-root user or you specify a non-default user when you run a container, by default the container will run as root. And it's easy to confirm that (unless you are set up with user namespaces) this is not just root inside the container but also root on the host machine.

This example assumes that you are using the docker command provided by Docker. If you have installed podman (*https://podman.io*), you may have followed the advice to alias docker so that it actually runs podman instead. The behavior of podman is quite different with regard to root users. I'll come to the differences later in this chapter, but for now be aware that the following example won't work with podman.

As a non-root user, run a shell inside an Alpine container using docker and check the user identity:

```
$ whoami
vagrant
$ docker run -it alpine sh
/ $ whoami
root
```

Even though it was a non-root user that ran the docker command to create a container, the user identity inside the identity is root. Now let's confirm that this is the same as root on the host by opening a second terminal on the same machine. Inside the container, run a sleep command:

```
/ $ sleep 100
```

In the second window, check the identity of this user:

```
$ ps -fC sleep
UID          PID  PPID  C STIME TTY          TIME CMD
root       30619 30557  0 16:44 pts/0    00:00:00 sleep 100
```

This process is owned by the root user from the host's perspective. Root inside the container is root on the host.

If you're using runc rather than docker to run containers, a similar demo would be less convincing because (aside from rootless containers, which we will discuss shortly) you need to be root on the host to run a container in the first place. This is because only root has sufficient capabilities to create namespaces, generally speaking. In Docker, it's the Docker daemon, running as root, that creates containers on your behalf.

Under Docker, the fact that containers run as root, even when initiated by a non-root user, is a form of privilege escalation. In and of itself, it's not necessarily a problem that the container is running as root, but it does ring alarm bells when thinking about security. If an attacker can escape a container that is running as root, they have full root access to the host, which means free access to everything on the machine. Do you want to be just one line of defense away from an attacker taking over a host?

Fortunately, it's possible to run containers as non-root users. You can either specify a non-root user ID or use the aforementioned rootless containers. Let's look at both of these options.

Override the User ID

You can override this at runtime by specifying a user ID for the container.

In runc, you can do this by modifying the *config.json* file inside the bundle. Change the process.user.uid, for example, like this:

```
    ...
    "process": {
            "terminal": true,
            "user": {
                    "uid": 5000,
                    ...
            }
            ...
    }
```

Now the runtime will pick up this user ID and use it for the container process:

```
$ sudo runc run sh
/ $ whoami
whoami: unknown uid 5000
/ $ sleep 100
```

Despite using sudo to run as root, the user ID for the container is 5000, and you can confirm this from the host:

```
$ ps -fC sleep
UID         PID PPID  C STIME TTY          TIME CMD
5000      26909 26893  0 16:16 pts/0     00:00:00 sleep 50
```

As you saw in Chapter 6, an OCI-compliant image bundle holds both the root filesystem for an image and the runtime configuration information. This same information is packed into a Docker image. You can override the user config with the --user option, like this:

```
$ docker run -it --user 5000 ubuntu bash
I have no name!@b7ca6ec82aa4:/$
```

You can change the user ID that is built into a Docker image with the USER command in its Dockerfile. But the vast majority of container images on public repositories are configured to use root because they don't have a USER setting. If there is no user ID specified, by default your container will run as root.

Root Requirement Inside Containers

There are many commonly used container images that encapsulate popular software that was originally designed to run directly on servers. Take the Nginx reverse proxy and load balancer, for example; it existed long before Docker became popular, but it's now available as a container image on Docker Hub. At least at the time of writing this book, the standard Nginx container image was configured to run as root by default. If you start an nginx container and look at the processes running within it, you will see the master process running as root:

```
$ docker run -d --name nginx nginx
4562ab6630747983e6d9c59d839aef95728b22a48f7aff3ad6b466dd70ebd0fe
$ docker top nginx
PID     USER    TIME            COMMAND
91413   root    0:00            nginx: master process nginx -g daemon off;
91458   101     0:00            nginx: worker process
```

It makes total sense for the nginx code to run as root when it's running on a server. By default it accepts requests on the traditional web port 80. Opening low-numbered ports (under 1024) requires the CAP_NET_BIND_SERVICE (see Chapter 2), and the simplest way to ensure this is true is to have nginx run as the root user. But this requirement makes a lot less sense in a container, where a port mapping means that the nginx code could listen on any port, and this could be mapped to port 80 (if required) on the host.

Recognizing that running as root is a problem, many vendors now provide Docker images that run as normal, unprivileged users. You will find a repository of Dockerfiles for Nginx, for example, at *https://github.com/nginxinc/docker-nginx-unprivileged*.

It's relatively straightforward to build an Nginx image that can run as a non-root user (there is a simple example here (*https://oreil.ly/UFmcG*)). For other applications, it can be trickier and may require changes to the code that are more extensive than a few tweaks to the Dockerfile and some configurations. Thankfully, Bitnami (*https://oreil.ly/W4nV2*) has gone to the trouble of creating and maintaining a series of non-root container images for many popular applications.

Another reason why container images are sometimes configured to run as root is so that they can install software using package managers like yum or apt. It's completely reasonable for this to happen *during the build of a container image*, but once the packages are installed, a later step in the Dockerfile could easily be a USER command so that the image is configured to run under a non-root user ID.

I strongly recommend that you don't allow containers to install software packages at runtime, for several reasons:

- It's inefficient: if you install all the software you need at build time, you do it once only, rather than repeating it every time you create a new instance of the container.
- Packages that get installed at runtime haven't been scanned for vulnerabilities (see Chapter 7).
- Related to the fact that the packages haven't been scanned, but arguably worse: it's harder to identify exactly what versions of packages are installed into each different running instance of your containers, so if you do become aware of a vulnerability, you won't know which containers to kill and redeploy.

- Depending on the application, you might be able to run the container as read-only (by using the `--read-only` option in `docker run`, or by setting `ReadOnly RootFileSystem` to true in a Kubernetes PodSecurityPolicy), which would make it harder for an attacker to install code.

- Adding packages at runtime means you are not treating them as immutable. See "Immutable Containers" on page 87 for more about the security advantages of immutable containers.

Another thing that you can do only as a root user is to modify the kernel. If you want to allow your containers to do this, be it on your own head!

 If you would like to explore the dangers of running as root under Kubernetes, you will find some demos at *https://github.com/lizrice/ running-with-scissors*.

For your own application code, use a non-root user whenever you can, or run with user namespaces (as seen in "User Namespace" on page 45), so that root inside the container is not the same as root on the host. One practical way to run with user namespaces, if your system supports it, is to use *rootless containers*.

Rootless Containers

If you worked through the examples in Chapter 4, you'll know that you need root privileges to perform some of the actions that go into creating a container. This is typically seen as a no-go in traditional shared machine environments, where multiple users can log in to the same machine. An example is a university system, where students and staff often have accounts on a shared machine or cluster of machines. System administrators quite rightly object to giving root privileges to a user so that they can create containers, as that would also allow them to do anything (deliberately or accidentally) to any other user's code or data.

In recent years, the Rootless Containers initiative (*https://rootlesscontaine.rs*) has been working on the kernel changes required to allow non-root users to run containers.

In a Docker system, you don't actually need to be root to run a container, but you need to be a member of the docker group that has permissions to send commands over the Docker socket to the Docker daemon. It's worth being aware that being able to do this *is equivalent to having root on the host*. Any member of that group can start a container, and as you are now aware, by default they will be running as root. If they were to mount the host's root directory with a command like docker run -v /:/host <image>, they would have full access to the host's root filesystem, too.

Rootless containers make use of the user namespace feature that you saw in "User Namespace" on page 45. A normal non-root user ID on the host can be mapped to root inside the container. If a container escape occurs somehow, the attacker doesn't automatically have root privileges, so this is a significant security enhancement.

The podman container implementation supports rootless containers, and it doesn't use a privileged daemon process in the way that Docker does. This is why the examples at the start of this chapter behave differently if you have docker aliased to podman.

Read more about root inside and outside a podman container in Scott McCarty's blog post (*https://oreil.ly/ISuFf*).

However, rootless containers aren't a panacea. Not every image that runs successfully as root in a normal container will behave the same in a rootless container, even though it appears to be running as root from the container's perspective. This is because of some subtleties in the way that Linux capabilities behave.

As the documentation (*https://oreil.ly/iZiaw*) for user namespaces states, they isolate not just user and group IDs but also other attributes, including capabilities. In other words, you can add or drop capabilities for a process in a user namespace, and they apply only inside that namespace. So if you add a capability for a rootless container, it applies only in that container, but not if the container is supposed to have access to other host resources.

Dan Walsh wrote a blog post (*https://oreil.ly/1fwZP*) with some good examples of this. One of them is about binding to low-numbered ports, which requires CAP_NET_BIND_SERVICE. If you run a normal container with CAP_NET_BIND_SERVICE (which it would likely have by default if running as root) and sharing the host's network namespace, it could bind to any host port. A rootless container, also with CAP_NET_BIND_SERVICE and sharing the host's network, would not be able to bind to low-numbered ports because the capability doesn't apply outside the container's user namespace.

By and large, the namespacing of capabilities is a good thing, as it allows container-ized processes to seemingly run as root, but without the ability to do things that would require capabilities at the system level, like changing the time or rebooting the machine. The vast majority of applications that can run in a normal container will also run successfully in a rootless container.

When using rootless containers, although the process appears from the container's perspective to be running as root, from the host's perspective it's a regular user. One interesting consequence of this is that the rootless container doesn't necessarily have the same file access permissions as it would have without the user remapping. To get around this, the filesystem needs to have support to remap file ownership and group ownership within the user namespace. (Not all filesystems have this support at the time of writing.)

As of this writing, rootless containers are still in their relative infancy. There is sup-port in runtimes, including `runc` and `podman`, and there is experimental support in Docker (*https://oreil.ly/GnOoq*). Irrespective of the runtime, using rootless containers is not yet an option in Kubernetes, though Akihiro Suda and others have built a proof of concept called Usernetes (*https://oreil.ly/42RRY*).

Running as root inside a container isn't exactly a problem in and of itself, as the attacker still needs to find a way to escape the container. From time to time container escape vulnerabilities have been found, and they probably will continue to be found. But a runtime vulnerability isn't the only way that container escape can be made pos-sible. Later in this chapter, you'll see ways in which risky container configurations can make it easy to escape the container, with no vulnerability required. Combine these bad configurations with containers running as root, and you have a recipe for disaster.

With user ID overrides and rootless containers, there are options for avoiding run-ning containers as the root user. However you achieve it, you should try to avoid con-tainers running as root.

The --privileged Flag and Capabilities

Docker and other container runtimes let you specify a `--privileged` option when you run a container. Andrew Martin has called it "the most dangerous flag in the history of computing," with good reason: it's incredibly powerful, and it's widely misunderstood.

It's often thought that `--privileged` equates to running a container as root, but you already know that containers run as root by default. So what other privileges could this flag be bestowing on the container?

The answer is that, although in Docker the process runs under the root user ID by default, a large group of root's normal Linux capabilities are not granted as a matter of course. (If you need a refresher on what capabilities are, skip back to "Linux Capabilities" on page 19.)

It's easy enough to see the capabilities that a container is granted by using the capsh utility, first in a container without --privileged and again with it (I have omitted some of the output for clarity):

```
vagrant@vagrant:~$ docker run --rm -it alpine sh -c 'apk add -U libcap; capsh
--print | grep Current'
...
Current: = cap_chown,cap_dac_override,cap_fowner,cap_fsetid,cap_kill,cap_setgid,
cap_setuid,cap_setpcap,cap_net_bind_service,cap_net_raw,cap_sys_chroot,cap_mknod,
cap_audit_write,cap_setfcap+eip

vagrant@vagrant:~$ docker run --rm -it --privileged alpine sh -c 'apk add -U
libcap; capsh --print | grep Current'
...
Current: = cap_chown,cap_dac_override,cap_dac_read_search,cap_fowner,cap_fsetid,
cap_kill,cap_setgid,cap_setuid,cap_setpcap,cap_linux_immutable,
cap_net_bind_service,cap_net_broadcast,cap_net_admin,cap_net_raw,cap_ipc_lock,
cap_ipc_owner,cap_sys_module,cap_sys_rawio,cap_sys_chroot,cap_sys_ptrace,
cap_sys_pacct,cap_sys_admin,cap_sys_boot,cap_sys_nice,cap_sys_resource,
cap_sys_time,cap_sys_tty_config,cap_mknod,cap_lease,cap_audit_write,
cap_audit_control,cap_setfcap,cap_mac_override,cap_mac_admin,cap_syslog,
cap_wake_alarm,cap_block_suspend,cap_audit_read+eip
```

The precise set of capabilities granted without the privileged flag is implementation dependent. The OCI defines a default set (*https://oreil.ly/ryVjj*), granted by runc.

That default set includes CAP_SYS_ADMIN, and this single capability flag grants access to a huge range of privileged activities, including things like manipulating namespaces and mounting filesystems.

> Eric Chiang wrote a blog post (*https://oreil.ly/4f4QO*) about the dangers of --privileged in which he shows an example of breaking out of a container onto the host filesystem by mounting a device from /dev into the container filesystem.

Docker introduced the --privileged flag to enable "Docker in Docker." This is used widely for build tools and CI/CD systems running as containers, which need access to the Docker daemon in order to use Docker to build container images. But as this blog post describes (*https://oreil.ly/-ULQo*), you should use Docker in Docker, and the --privileged flag in general, with caution.

A more subtle reason why the --privileged flag is so dangerous is that, because people often think that it's needed to give the container root privileges, they also believe

---

the converse: that a container running without this flag is not a root process. Please refer back to "Containers Run as Root by Default" on page 105 if you're not yet convinced about this.

Even if you have reasons to run containers with the `--privileged` flag, I would advise controls or at least an audit to ensure that only those containers that really need it are granted the flag. Consider specifying individual capabilities instead.

The Tracee (*https://oreil.ly/1dQof*) tool that I mentioned in Chapter 8 can be used to trace out `cap_capable` events, showing the capabilities that a given container requests from the kernel.

Here is example output showing the first few events traced from a container running nginx, with some output removed for clarity.

Terminal 1:

```
$ docker run -it --rm nginx
```

Terminal 2:

```
root@vagrant$ ./tracee.py -c -e cap_capable
TIME(s)   UTS_NAME      UID  EVENT         COMM    PID  PPID  RET  ARGS
125.000   c8520fe719e5  0    cap_capable   nginx   6    1     0    CAP_SETGID
125.000   c8520fe719e5  0    cap_capable   nginx   6    1     0    CAP_SETGID
125.000   c8520fe719e5  0    cap_capable   nginx   6    1     0    CAP_SETUID
124.964   c8520fe719e5  0    cap_capable   nginx   1    3500  0    CAP_SYS_ADMIN
124.964   c8520fe719e5  0    cap_capable   nginx   1    3500  0    CAP_SYS_ADMIN
```

Once you know which capabilities your container needs, you can follow the principle of least privilege and specify at runtime the precise set that should be granted. The recommended approach is to drop all capabilities and then add back the necessary ones as follows:

```
$ docker run --cap-drop=all --cap-add=<cap1> --cap-add=<cap2> <image> ...
```

Now you are warned of the dangers of the `--privileged` flag and the opportunity to shrink-wrap capabilities for a container. Let's look at another way that container isolation can be sidestepped: mounting sensitive directories from the host.

Mounting Sensitive Directories

Using the `-v` option, you can mount a host directory into a container so that it is available from the container. And there is nothing to stop you from mounting the host's root directory into a container, like this:

```
$ touch /ROOT_FOR_HOST
$ docker run -it -v /:/hostroot ubuntu bash
root@91083a4eca7d:/$ ls /
bin   dev  home      lib     media  opt   root  sbin  sys  usr
```

```
boot  etc  hostroot  lib64  mnt    proc  run   srv   tmp  var
root@91083a4eca7d:/$ ls /hostroot/
ROOT_FOR_HOST  etc         lib        media  root  srv  vagrant
bin            home        lib64      mnt    run   sys  var
...
```

An attacker who compromises this container is root on the host, with full access to the entire host filesystem.

Mounting the entire filesystem is a pathological example, but there are plenty of other examples that range in their subtlety, such as the following:

- Mounting /etc would permit modifying the host's /etc/passwd file from within the container, or messing with `cron` jobs, or `init`, or `systemd`.

- Mounting /bin or similar directories such as /usr/bin or /usr/sbin would allow the container to write executables into the host directory—including overwriting existing executables.

- Mounting host log directories into a container could enable an attacker to modify the logs to erase traces of their dastardly deeds on that host.

- In a Kubernetes environment, mounting /var/log can give access to the entire host filesystem to any user who has access to `kubectl logs`. This is because container log files are symlinks from /var/log to elsewhere in the filesystem, but there is nothing to stop the container from pointing the symlink at any other file. See this blog post (*https://oreil.ly/gN7no*) for more on this interesting escape.

Mounting the Docker Socket

In a Docker environment, there is a Docker daemon process that essentially does all the work. When you run the `docker` command-line utility, this sends instructions to the daemon over the Docker socket that lives at /var/run/docker.sock. Any entity that can write to that socket can also send instructions to the Docker daemon. The daemon runs as root and will happily build and run any software of your choosing on your behalf, including—as you have seen—running a container as root on the host. Thus, access to the Docker socket is effectively the equivalent of root access on the host.

One very common use of mounting the Docker socket is in CI tools like Jenkins, where the socket is needed specifically for sending instructions to Docker to run image builds as part of your pipeline. This is a legitimate thing to do, but it does create a potential soft underbelly that an attacker can pierce. A user who can modify a Jenkinsfile can get Docker to run commands, including those that could give the user root access to the underlying cluster. For this reason, it's exceptionally bad practice to run a CI/CD pipeline that mounts a Docker socket in a production cluster.

Sharing Namespaces Between a Container and Its Host

On occasion there might be reasons to have a container use some of the same namespaces as its host. For example, suppose you want to run a process in a Docker container but give it access to the process information from the host. In Docker, you can request this with the --pid=host parameter.

Recall that containerized processes are all visible from the host; thus, sharing the process namespace to a container lets that container see the other containerized processes, too. The following example starts by running a long-running sleep inside one container; that process can be observed from another container started with --pid=host:

```
vagrant@vagrant$ docker run --name sleep --rm -d alpine sleep 1000
fa19f51fe07fca8d60454cf8ee32b7e8b7b60b73128e13f6a01751c601280110
vagrant@vagrant$ docker run --pid=host --name alpine --rm -it alpine sh
/ $ ps | grep sleep
30575 root      0:00 sleep 1000
30738 root      0:00 grep sleep
/ $
```

What's even more exciting is that running kill -9 <pid> from the second container can kill the sleep process in the first!

You have seen several ways in which sharing namespaces or volumes between containers, or between a container and its host, can weaken the container's isolation and compromise security, but it's by no means *always* a bad idea to share information with containers. To conclude this chapter, let's look at sidecar containers, which are a common pattern use for good reasons.

Sidecar Containers

A *sidecar container* is deliberately given access to one or more of an application container's namespaces so that it can offload functionality from that application. In a microservice architecture, you might have functionality that you want to reuse in all your microservices, and a common pattern is to package that functionality into sidecar container images so that it can easily be reused. Here are a few common examples:

- Service mesh sidecars take over the networking functionality on behalf of the application container. The service mesh can, for example, ensure that all network connections use mutual TLS. Offloading this functionality to a sidecar means that so long as a container is deployed with the sidecar, it will set up secure TLS connections; there is no need for each application team to spend time enabling this in its application code. (Further discussion of service meshes is coming up in the next chapter—see "Service Mesh" on page 129.)

- Observability sidecars can set up destinations and configurations for logging, tracing, and gathering metrics. For example, Prometheus (*https://oreil.ly/Jn10W*) and OpenTelemetry (*https://oreil.ly/0HwpE*) support sidecars for exporting observability data.

- Security sidecars can police the executables and network connections that are permitted within an application container. (For example, see my blog post (*https://oreil.ly/oHAEk*) about securing AWS Fargate containers using Aqua's MicroEnforcer in sidecar containers, or a similar solution from Twistlock (*https://oreil.ly/5YHQk*).)

This is just a selection of applications for sidecar containers, which legitimately share namespaces with application containers.

Summary

This chapter covered several ways in which the isolation that's normally provided by containers can be compromised through bad configuration.

All the configuration options are provided for good reasons. For example, mounting host directories into a container can be extremely useful, and sometimes you do need the option to run a container as root or even with the additional capabilities provided by the `--privileged` flag. However, if you're concerned about security, you'll want to minimize the extent to which these potentially dangerous configurations are used and employ tools to spot when they are happening.

If you're running in any kind of multitenant environment, you should be even more attentive to containers with these potentially dangerous configurations. Any `--privileged` container will have full access to any other container on the same host, regardless of relatively superficial controls such as whether they are running in the same Kubernetes namespace.

In "Sidecar Containers" on page 115, I mentioned service meshes, which can offload some networking functionality. Now seems like a good time to talk about container networking.

CHAPTER 10

Container Network Security

Every external attack reaches your deployment across a network, so it's important to understand something about networking in order to consider how to secure your applications and data. This isn't going to be a comprehensive treatment of everything to do with networking (that would make this book a lot longer!), but it should give you the essentials of a sensible mental model you can use to think about network security in your container deployment.

I'll start with an overview of container firewalling, which can provide a much more granular approach to network security than traditional firewalling approaches.

Then there is a review of the seven-layer networking model, which is worth knowing about so that you can understand the level a network security feature acts at. With this in place, we will discuss how container firewalling is implemented and look at some best practices for network policy rules. We end the chapter by looking at the network security features of service meshes.

Container Firewalls

Containers often go hand in hand with microservice architectures, where an application is broken into small components that can be deployed independently of each other. This can offer real benefits from a security perspective, because it's much easier to define what normal behavior looks like in a small component. A given container probably has to communicate with only a limited set of other containers, and only a subset of containers need contact with the outside world.

For example, consider an ecommerce application broken into microservices. One of these microservices could handle product search requests; it receives search requests from end users and looks up their search queries in a product database. The containers that make up this service don't have any reason to communicate with, say, the payment gateway. Figure 10-1 illustrates this example.

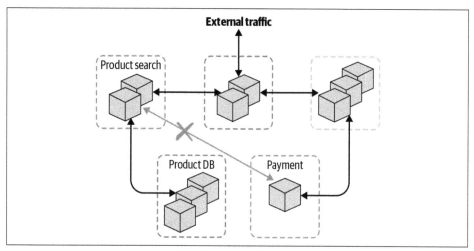

Figure 10-1. Container firewalling

A container firewall can restrict the traffic that flows to and from a set of containers. In an orchestrator like Kubernetes, the term "container firewall" is rarely used; instead, you'll hear about network policies being enforced by a network plug-in. In both cases, the principle is to restrict container network traffic so that it can only flow to and from approved destinations. A container firewall (like its traditional counterpart) will typically also report on attempted connections outside the rules, providing useful forensics for investigation into possible attacks.

Container firewalls can be used in conjunction with other network security tools that you may have come across in traditional deployments as well. For example:

- It's very common to deploy your container environment in a Virtual Private Cloud (VPC), which isolates your hosts from the rest of the world.
- You can use a firewall around the entire cluster to control traffic in and out.
- You can use API firewalls (also known as WAF, or Web Application Firewalls) to restrict traffic at Layer 7.

None of these approaches are new. Combining them with container-aware security gives additional defense in depth.

Before we look at how container firewalling is achieved, let's review the seven-layer networking model and follow the path of an IP packet through a network.

OSI Networking Model

The Open Systems Interconnection (OSI) networking model was published in 1984 and defines a layered model of networking that is still commonly referenced today, although, as you can see from Figure 10-2, the seven layers don't all have an equivalent in IP-based networks.

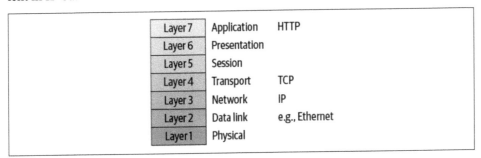

Layer 7	Application	HTTP
Layer 6	Presentation	
Layer 5	Session	
Layer 4	Transport	TCP
Layer 3	Network	IP
Layer 2	Data link	e.g., Ethernet
Layer 1	Physical	

Figure 10-2. OSI model

- Layer 7 is the application layer. If you think about an application making a web request or sending a RESTful API request, you are picturing something that happens at Layer 7. The request is typically addressed by a URL, and to get the request to its destination, the domain name gets mapped to an Internet Protocol (IP) address using a protocol called Domain Name Resolution that is offered by a Domain Name Service (DNS).

- Layer 4 is the transport layer, typically TCP or UDP packets. This is the layer at which port numbers apply.

- Layer 3 is the layer at which IP packets travel and at which IP routers operate. An IP network has a set of IP addresses assigned to it, and when a container joins the network it gets assigned one of those IP addresses. For the purposes of this chapter, it doesn't matter whether the IP network uses IP v4 or IP v6—you can consider that to be an implementation detail.

- At Layer 2, data packets are addressed to endpoints connected to a physical or virtual interface (which I'll discuss in a moment). There are several Layer 2 protocols, including Ethernet, WiFi, and, if you cast your mind back into history, Token Ring. (WiFi is slightly confusing here since it covers both Layer 2 and Layer 1.) I'll only cover Ethernet in this chapter since that is predominantly what's used for Layer 2 container networking. At Layer 2, interfaces are addressed using MAC addresses.

- Layer 1 is called the physical layer, although to keep us all on our toes, interfaces at Layer 1 can be virtual. A physical machine will have a physical network device attached to some kind of cable or wireless transmitter. Cast your mind back to Chapter 5, and you will recall that a VMM gives a guest kernel access to virtual devices that map to these physical devices. When you get a network interface on, say, an EC2 instance in AWS, you're getting access to one of these virtual interfaces. Container network interfaces are commonly virtual at Layer 1 as well. Whenever a container joins a network, it has a Layer 1 interface to that network.

Let's see what happens at these different layers when an application wants to send a message.

Sending an IP Packet

Imagine an application that wants to send a request to a destination URL. Since this is the application, it stands to reason from the preceding definition that this is happening at Layer 7.

The first step is a DNS look-up to find the IP address that corresponds to the host name in that URL. DNS could be defined locally (as in the */etc/hosts* file on your laptop), or it could be resolved by making a DNS request to a remote service at a configured IP address. (If the application already knows the IP address it wants to send a message to, rather than using a URL, the DNS step is skipped.)

Once the networking stack knows which destination IP address it needs to send the packet to, the next step is a Layer 3 routing decision, which consists of two parts:

1. To reach a given destination, there might be multiple hops in the IP network. Given the destination IP address, what is the IP address of the next hop?
2. What interface corresponds to this next-hop IP address?

Next, the packet has to be converted to Ethernet frames, and the next-hop IP address has to be mapped to the corresponding MAC address. This relies on the Address Resolution Protocol (ARP), which maps IP addresses to MAC addresses. If the network stack doesn't already know the MAC address for the next-hop IP address (which could already be held in an ARP cache), then it uses ARP to find out.

Once the network stack has the next-hop MAC address, the message can be sent out over the interface. Depending on the network implementation, this could be a point-to-point connection, or the interface may be connected to a *bridge.*

The easiest way to understand a bridge is to imagine a physical device with a number of Ethernet cables plugged in. The other end of each cable connects to the network card on a device—a computer, say. Every physical network card has a unique MAC address hardcoded into it by the manufacturer. The bridge learns the MAC address at the far end of each of the cables plugged into its interface. All the devices connected to the bridge can send packets to each other through the bridge. In container networking the bridge is implemented in software rather than being a separate physical device, and the Ethernet cables are replaced by virtual Ethernet interfaces. So the message arrives at the bridge, which uses the next-hop MAC address to decide which interface to forward it on.

When the message arrives at the other end of the Ethernet connection, the IP packet is extracted and passed back up to Layer 3. Data is encapsulated with headers at different layers in the networking stack, as shown in Figure 10-3.

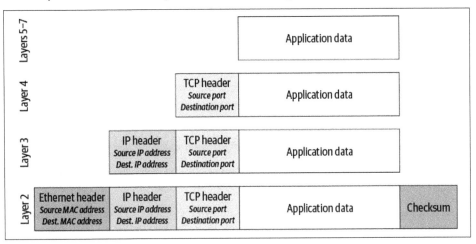

Figure 10-3. Networking headers

If this is the packet's final destination, then it gets passed up to the receiving application. However, this might just be the next hop for the packet, and in that case the networking stack needs to make another routing decision to decide where to send the packet next.

This explanation glosses over a few details (such as how ARP works, or how routing decides which is the next-hop IP address), but it should be sufficient for our purposes of thinking about container networking.

IP Addresses for Containers

The previous section talks about getting traffic to reach a destination based on its IP address. Containers can share the IP address of their host, or they can each have their own network stack running in their own network namespace. You saw how network namespaces are set up in Chapter 4. Since there's a good chance you are running containers under Kubernetes, let's explore how IP addresses are used in Kubernetes.

In Kubernetes, each pod has its own IP address. If the pod includes more than one container, you can infer that each container shares the same IP address. This is achieved by having all containers in a pod share the same network namespace. Every node is configured to use a range of addresses (a CIDR block), and when a pod is scheduled to a node, it gets assigned one of the addresses from that range.

It's not strictly true that nodes are always assigned a range of addresses up-front. For example, on AWS, a pluggable IP address management module dynamically assigns pod IP addresses from the range associated with the underlying VPC.

Kubernetes requires that pods in a cluster can connect directly to each other without any Network Address Translation (NAT) between them. In other circumstances, NAT allows IP addresses to be mapped so that one entity sees a destination as being at a certain IP address, even though that isn't the actual address of the destination device. (This is one reason why IPv4 has been in use for much longer than originally predicted. Although the number of IP-addressable devices has far outstripped available addresses in the IPv4 address space, NAT means we can reuse the vast majority of IP addresses within private networks.) In Kubernetes, network security policies and segmentation might prevent a pod from being able to communicate with another pod, but if the two pods can communicate, they see each other's IP addresses transparently without any NAT mapping. There can, however, still be NAT between pods and the outside world.

Kubernetes services are a form of NAT. A Kubernetes service is a resource in its own right, and it gets assigned an IP address of its own. It's just an IP address though—a service doesn't have any interfaces, and it doesn't actually listen for or send traffic. The address is just used for routing purposes. The service is associated with some number of pods that actually do the work of the service, so packets sent to the service IP address need to be forwarded to one of these pods. We'll shortly see how this is done through rules at Layer 3.

Network Isolation

It's worth explicitly pointing out that two components can communicate with each other only if they are connected to the same network. In traditional host-based environments, you might have isolated different applications from each other by having separate VLANs for each one.

In the container world, Docker made it easy to set up multiple networks using the docker network command, but it's not something that fits naturally in the Kubernetes model where every pod can (modulo network policies and security tools) access every other pod by IP address.

It's also worth noting that in Kubernetes the control components run in pods and are all connected to the same network as the application pods. If you come from a telecommunications background, this may surprise you, since a lot of effort was put into separating the control plane from the data plane in phone networks, primarily for security reasons.

Instead, Kubernetes container networking is enforced using network policies (*https://oreil.ly/sHh4p*) that act at Layer 3/4.

Layer 3/4 Routing and Rules

As you already know, routing at Layer 3 is concerned about deciding the next hop for an IP packet. This decision is based on a set of rules about which addresses are reached over which interface. But this is just a subset of things you can do with Layer 3 rules: there are also some fun things that can go on at this level to drop packets or manipulate IP addresses, for example, to implement load balancing, NAT, firewalls, and network security policies. Rules can also act at layer 4 to take into account the port number. These rules rely on a kernel feature called `netfilter` (*https://netfilter.org*).

`netfilter` is a packet-filtering framework that was first introduced into the Linux kernel in version 2.4. It uses a set of rules that define what to do with a packet based on its source and destination addresses.

There are a few different ways that `netfilter` rules can be configured in user space. Let's look at the two most common options: `iptables` and IPVS.

iptables

The `iptables` tool is one way of configuring IP packet–handling rules that are dealt with in the kernel using `netfilter`. There are several different table types; the two most interesting types in the context of container networking are filter and nat:

- filter—for deciding whether to drop or forward packets
- nat—for translating addresses

As a root user, you can see the current set of rules of a particular type by running `iptables -t <table type> -L`.

The `netfilter` rules that you can set up with `iptables` can be very useful for security purposes. Several container firewall solutions, as well as Kubernetes network plugins, make use of `iptables` to set up sophisticated network policy rules that are implemented using `netfilter` rules. I'll come back to this in "Network Policies" on page 125. First, let's delve into the rules that get set up with `iptables`.

In Kubernetes, kube-proxy uses `iptables` rules to handle the load balancing of traffic to services. As mentioned earlier, a service is an abstraction that maps a service name to a set of pods. The service name gets resolved to an IP address using DNS. When a packet destined for that service IP address arrives, there is an `iptables` rule that matches the destination address and swaps the destination address for that of one of the corresponding pods. If the set of pods behind a service changes, the `iptables` rules get rewritten on each host accordingly.

It's easy enough to see the `iptables` rules for a service. Let's take a Kubernetes cluster with a two-replica deployment of `nginx`, behind a service (I have removed some of the output fields for clarity):

```
$ kubectl get svc,pods -o wide
NAME                    TYPE        CLUSTER-IP      PORT(S)
service/kubernetes      ClusterIP   10.96.0.1       443/TCP
service/my-nginx        NodePort    10.100.132.10   8080:32144/TCP

NAME                            READY   STATUS    IP
pod/my-nginx-75897978cd-n5rdv   1/1     Running   10.32.0.4
pod/my-nginx-75897978cd-ncnfk   1/1     Running   10.32.0.3
```

You can list the current address translation rules with `iptables -t nat -L`. There will likely be a lot of output, but it's not too hard to find the interesting parts that correspond to this `nginx` service. First, here is the rule that corresponds to the `my-nginx` service running on IP address 10.100.132.10. You can see that it's part of a chain called "KUBE-SERVICES," which makes sense since it relates to a service:

```
Chain KUBE-SERVICES (2 references)
target                     prot opt source       destination
...
KUBE-SVC-SV7AMNAGZFKZEMQ4  tcp  --  anywhere     10.100.132.10   /* default/my-
nginx:http cluster IP */ tcp dpt:http-alt
...
```

The rule specifies a target chain, which appears later in the `iptables` rules:

```
Chain KUBE-SVC-SV7AMNAGZFKZEMQ4 (2 references)
target                     prot opt source       destination
KUBE-SEP-XZGVVMRRSKK6PWWN  all  --  anywhere     anywhere     statistic mode
random probability 0.50000000000
KUBE-SEP-PUXUHBP3DTPPX72C  all  --  anywhere     anywhere
```

It seems reasonable to infer from this that traffic is being split between these two targets with equal probability. This makes a lot of sense when you see that these targets have rules that correspond to the IP addresses of the pods (10.32.0.3 and 10.32.0.4):

```
Chain KUBE-SEP-XZGVVMRRSKK6PWWN (1 references)
target           prot opt source              destination
KUBE-MARK-MASQ   all  --  10.32.0.3           anywhere
DNAT             tcp  --  anywhere            anywhere       tcp to:10.32.0.3:80
...
Chain KUBE-SEP-PUXUHBP3DTPPX72C (1 references)
target           prot opt source              destination
KUBE-MARK-MASQ   all  --  10.32.0.4           anywhere
DNAT             tcp  --  anywhere            anywhere       tcp to:10.32.0.4:80
```

The problem with `iptables` is that if you have a lot of complex sets of rules on each host, performance may drop off. In fact, kube-proxy's use of `iptables` was identified as a performance bottleneck when running Kubernetes at scale. This blog post (*https://oreil.ly/xOyqb*) points out that 2,000 services with 10 pods each results in an additional 20,000 `iptables` rules on every node. To address this, Kubernetes can now use IPVS for load-balancing services.

IPVS

IP Virtual Server (IPVS) is sometimes referred to as Layer 4 load balancing or Layer 4 LAN switching. It is another rules implementation similar to `iptables`, but it's optimized for load balancing by storing the forwarding rules in hash tables.

This optimization makes it very performant for kube-proxy's use case, but it doesn't necessarily mean you can draw conclusions about the performance of network plugins implementing network policies.

Project Calico published a performance comparison of `iptables` and IPVS (*https://oreil.ly/xGO0N*).

Whether it's IPVS or `iptables` that manages `netfilter` rules, they act within the kernel. Recalling that the kernel is shared across all the containers on a host, this tells you that when they are used to enforce security policies, this is happening at the host level and not within each container.

Now that you have an idea how `netfilter` rules are manipulated, let's see how they are used to implement networking policies for security purposes.

Network Policies

There are various solutions that apply network policies in both Kubernetes and other container deployments. Outside Kubernetes they might be called "container firewalls" or "network microsegmentation," but the basic principles are the same.

Network policies in Kubernetes define the traffic that can flow to and from different pods. Policies can be defined in terms of ports, IP addresses, services, or labeled pods. When a message is going to be sent or received, if it's not approved by the policy, the network needs to either refuse to set up a connection or drop the message packets. In the ecommerce example from the start of this chapter, one policy might prevent traffic from the product search container that has the destination address of the payment service.

Many network policy implementations make use of `netfilter` rules for their implementation. Let's take a look at a Kubernetes network policy rule as implemented in `iptables`. Here's a simple NetworkPolicy object that allows pods to access the `my-nginx` service only if they are labeled with `access=true`:

```
apiVersion: networking.k8s.io/v1
kind: NetworkPolicy
metadata:
  name: access-nginx
spec:
  podSelector:
    matchLabels:
      app: my-nginx
  ingress:
  - from:
    - podSelector:
        matchLabels:
          access: "true"
```

Creating this network policy results in the following additional `iptables` rule in the filter table:

```
Chain WEAVE-NPC-INGRESS (1 references)
target     prot opt source        destination
ACCEPT     all  -- anywhere       anywhere              match-set weave-{U;]TI.l|Md
RzDhN7$NRn[t]d src match-set weave-vC070kAfB$if8}PFMX{V9Mv2m dst /* pods: namespa
ce: default, selector: access=true -> pods: namespace: default, selector: app=my-
nginx (ingress) */
```

It's the networking plug-in (*https://oreil.ly/VmVCc*), rather than a core Kubernetes component, that creates `iptables` rules to match the network policy. In the preceding example, as you can probably guess from the chain name, I was using Weave as the networking plug-in. The match-set rule isn't really human-readable, but the comment matches our expectation that the rule allows traffic from pods in the default namespace with the label `access=true`, going to pods in the default namespace with the label `app=my-nginx`.

Now that you have seen Kubernetes using `iptables` rules for network policy enforcement, let's try configuring a rule of our own. I'm doing this on a fresh Ubuntu installation so that the rules are empty to start with:

```
$ sudo iptables -L
Chain INPUT (policy ACCEPT)
target     prot opt source            destination

Chain FORWARD (policy ACCEPT)
target     prot opt source            destination

Chain OUTPUT (policy ACCEPT)
target     prot opt source            destination
```

I'll set up `netcat` to respond to requests on port 8000:

```
$ while true; do  echo "hello world" | nc -l 8000 -N; done
```

In another terminal I can now send requests to this port:

```
$ curl localhost:8000
hello world
```

Now I'll create an `iptables` rule that rejects traffic on port 8000:

```
$ sudo iptables -I INPUT -j REJECT -p tcp --dport=8000
$ sudo iptables -L
Chain INPUT (policy ACCEPT)
target     prot opt source       destination
REJECT     tcp  --  anywhere     anywhere            tcp dpt:8000 reject-with icmp-
port-unreachable

Chain FORWARD (policy ACCEPT)
target     prot opt source       destination

Chain OUTPUT (policy ACCEPT)
target     prot opt source       destination
```

As you probably would have predicted, the `curl` command no longer succeeds in getting a response:

```
$ curl localhost:8000
curl: (7) Failed to connect to localhost port 8000: Connection refused
```

This demonstrates that `iptables` can be used to restrict traffic. You could imagine building up lots of rules like this to limit the traffic between containers, but I don't recommend doing it by hand. In practice you probably want to use a preexisting implementation rather than writing your own container network security policy directly in `iptables` rules. You'll get an easier-to-use interface for configuring policies, rather than having to create rules from scratch, and in a multi-node system you'll have different rules on each node. And there will be a lot of rules—to give you an idea, I have a single Kubernetes node running the Calico network plug-in, and with just a handful of application pods running and no network policies, `iptables -L` on this machine gives me over 300 lines of filter table rules. The rules themselves are high performance, but writing them is a complex task. Also, containers tend to be ephemeral, so the rules need to be rewritten as containers are created and destroyed. This is manageable only when the rules are automated rather than written by hand.

Network Policy Solutions

So what can you use to provide this automation? Kubernetes has NetworkPolicy objects, although as mentioned earlier, Kubernetes does not itself enforce them. They have effect only when you're using a network plug-in (*https://oreil.ly/Bv_JG*) that supports them. Depending on the network plug-in, you may have options for upgrading to a commercial version that gives you more flexibility or easier management.

Some commercial container security platforms include container firewalls that achieve essentially the same thing but are not installed directly as a Kubernetes network plug-in. These can include the ability to learn what normal traffic looks like for a particular container image so that the policy can be created automatically.

Network Policy Best Practices

Whichever tooling you use to create, manage, and enforce network policies, there are some recommended best practices:

Default deny
> Following the principle of least privilege, set up a policy for each namespace that denies ingress traffic by default (*https://oreil.ly/L6OjC*) and then add policies to permit traffic only where you expect it.

Default deny egress
> Egress policies relate to traffic exiting your pod. If a container were to be compromised, an attacker could probe the surrounding environment across the network. Set up policies for each namespace to deny egress traffic by default (*https://oreil.ly/RmeUT*) and then add policies for expected egress traffic.

Restrict pod-to-pod traffic
> Pods are typically labeled to indicate their application. Use policies to limit traffic so that it can only flow between permitted applications, along with policies that allow traffic only from pods with the appropriate labels.

Restrict ports
> Restrict traffic so that it is accepted only to specific ports for each application.

> Ahmet Alp Balkan provides a set of useful network policy recipes (*https://oreil.ly/JogsQ*).

The network policies that I have discussed so far act at the lower levels of the networking stack (up to Layer 4). Now let's consider service meshes, which act at the application layers.

Service Mesh

A *service mesh* provides an additional set of controls and capabilities for how applications connect with each other that are implemented at the application layer (Layers 5–7 in the OSI model you saw at the start of this chapter).

There are a few different service mesh projects and products in the cloud native ecosystem, including Istio, Envoy, and Linkerd, and managed options from the cloud providers such as AWS App Mesh. Service meshes offer several features and benefits, some of which relate to security.

The way a service mesh typically works in Kubernetes is for it to be injected as a sidecar container into each application pod and then the sidecar handles networking on behalf of the other container(s) in the pod. All traffic to and from the pod goes via this sidecar proxy. Rule enforcement happens in user space within the proxy.

The service mesh can be configured to use mutual TLS in these sidecar proxies. This gives the benefit of secure, encrypted connections within the deployment, making it much harder for an attacker to intercept traffic even if they manage to find a foothold within the deployment. If you're not already familiar with mTLS, it's coming up in Chapter 11.

Service meshes also typically provide options to enforce application-layer network policies so that the pods in a service can communicate with other (internal or external) services only if the policy permits it. Because they act at the application, there is a clear separation of concerns between these policies and the Layer 1–4 network policies considered earlier in this chapter.

> The Istio documentation provides an example of an application-layer isolation policy (*https://oreil.ly/6bUHM*) where traffic is allowed to flow only from ingress to a specific port on pods from a particular application.

The mutual TLS and policy support are powerful security benefits provided by a service mesh, but there are two things to be aware of:

- A service mesh can provide security support only to pods into which it has been injected as a sidecar. If it's not present, it can't do anything.
- Because service mesh network policies are defined at the service level, they are not effective at protecting your underlying infrastructure from a compromised pod.

The best practice for enterprises is to use the principle of defense in depth. Alongside a service mesh, it would be a good idea to have tooling in place to confirm that the sidecar is present in all containers, and to use a complementary container network security solution that can prevent/restrict any traffic that flows directly between containers, or between containers and external addresses, rather than via a service IP address.

 There are other features that service meshes may offer, such as canary deployments, that are unrelated to networking or security. For more information, see this article (*https://oreil.ly/0Fq5A*) from DigitalOcean.

A service mesh sidecar container lives alongside application containers within a pod. If an application container were to be compromised, it might attempt to bypass or modify the rules enforced by the sidecar. The sidecar and application containers share the same network namespace; thus it is a good idea to make sure that the CAP_NET_ADMIN capability is withheld from application containers so that if one is compromised, it can't modify the shared networking stack.

Summary

In this chapter, you have seen how containers enable very granular firewalling solutions within a deployment. This granularity helps maintain several security principles:

- Segregation of duties/least privilege by allowing containers only a limited ability to communicate.
- Limiting the blast radius by preventing a compromised container from attacking all its neighbors.
- Defense in depth by combining container firewalls with service meshes and cluster-wide traditional firewalling.

I mentioned that service meshes can automatically set up mutual TLS connections between containers. In the next chapter, I will explain how TLS makes communications more secure, and attempt to demystify the role of keys and certificates in setting up these secure connections.

Securely Connecting Components with TLS

In any distributed system, there are different components that need to communicate with each other, and in a cloud native world those components may well be containers exchanging messages with each other or with other internal or external components. In this chapter, you'll see how secured transport connections allow components to safely send encrypted messages to each other. You'll explore how components identify themselves to each other and set up secure connections between themselves so that malicious components can't get involved in these communications.

If you're familiar with how keys and certificates work, you can safely skip this chapter, as there is nothing particularly container-specific about it. I have included it in this book because in my experience, it's an area of confusion for many folks who may be coming across these concepts for the first time when they start exploring containers and cloud native tools.

If you are responsible for administering a cloud native system, you will likely need to configure certificates, keys, and certificate authorities for Kubernetes, etcd, or other infrastructure components. These can be notoriously confusing, and installation instructions tend to explain what to do without covering the "why" or the "how." You may find this chapter useful for understanding the roles that these different pieces play.

Let's start by considering what we mean by "secure connections."

Secure Connections

In everyday life, we see secure connections being used in web browsers. If you browse to, say, your online banking facility and you don't see a little green padlock, you know that the connection isn't secure, so you shouldn't enter your login credentials. There are two parts to setting up a secure connection to a website:

- First, you need to know that the website you are browsing is really owned by your bank. Your browser checks the identity of the website by verifying its certificate.

- The second part is encryption. When you are accessing your bank information, you don't want any third parties to be able to intercept (or worse, interfere with) that communication channel.

You may well be familiar with the fact that secure website connections use a protocol called *HTTPS*, which stands for HTTP-Secure. As its name suggests, this is a regular HTTP connection that has been made secure, and this security is added at the transport layer using a protocol imaginatively called *transport layer security* (TLS).

If you're thinking, "But I thought the *S* stood for SSL, or Secure Sockets Layer?" don't worry—you're really not wrong. The transport layer is the layer that communicates between a pair of network sockets, and TLS is the modern name for the protocol that used to be called SSL. The first SSL spec was published by Netscape in 1995 (as version 2, the initial version 1 having been recognized as so seriously flawed that it was never released). By 1999, the Internet Engineering Task Force (IETF) created the TLS v1.0 standard, largely based on Netscape's SSL v3.0, and the industry is now primarily using TLS v1.3.

Whether you call it SSL or TLS, the protocol relies on certificates to set up secure connections. Confusingly, we still tend to call these "SSL certificates" 20 years after the move to TLS. If you really want to be correct, you should call them "X.509 certificates."

Both identity and encryption key information can be exchanged using X.509 certificates. Let's delve into what these certificates are and how they work.

 There are several tools for generating keys, certificates, and certificate authorities including ssh-keygen, openssl keygen, and minica. I demonstrated using minica in a talk called "A Go Programmer's Guide to Secure Connections" (*https://youtu.be/ OF3TM-b890E*) in which I also show what's happening step-by-step as a client sets up a TLS connection with a server.

X.509 Certificates

The term "X.509" is the name of the International Telecommunications Union (ITU) standard that defines these certificates. The certificate is a piece of structured data that includes information about the identity of its owner and also includes the public encryption key for communicating with the owner. This public key is half of a public/ private key pair.

This is to certify that

my-name

has public key

abcdef

CA

expires MM-DD-YYYY

Figure 11-1. Certificate

As illustrated in Figure 11-1, the vital pieces of information in a certificate are:

- The name of the entity that this certificate identifies. This entity is called the *subject*, and the subject name is typically in the form of a domain name. In practice, certificates should use a field called "Subject Alternative Names" that allows the certificate to identify the subject by more than one name.

- The subject's public key.

- The name of the certificate authority that issued the certificate. I'll come back to this later in this chapter, in "Certificate Authorities" on page 134.

- The validity of the certificate—that is, the date and time at which the certificate expires.

Public/Private Key Pairs

As its name suggests, a public key can be shared with anyone. The public key has a corresponding private key that the owner should never disclose.

The math behind the encryption and decryption is beyond the scope of this book, but I collected some recommended resources about it in a post on Medium (*https://oreil.ly/Tbhvd*).

The private key is generated first, and from that, a corresponding public key can be calculated. The public/private key pair can be used for two very useful purposes:

- As illustrated in Figure 11-2, a public key can be used to encrypt a message that can only be decrypted by the holder of the corresponding private key.

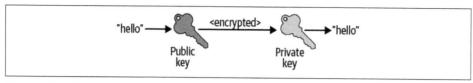

Figure 11-2. Encryption

- A private key can be used to sign a message that any holder of the corresponding public key can check to verify that it came from the private key owner. This is shown in Figure 11-3.

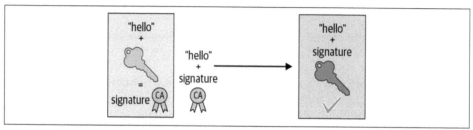

Figure 11-3. Signing

Both the encryption and the signing capabilities of public/private key pairs are used to set up secure connections.

Let's suppose that you and I want to exchange encrypted messages. Once I have generated a key pair, I can give you the public key so that you can send me encrypted messages. But if I send you that public key, how do you know that it really came from me and not from an imposter? To establish that I am who I say am, we will need to involve a third party that you trust, and that will vouch for my identity. This is the function of a *certificate authority*.

Certificate Authorities

A certificate authority, or CA, is a trusted entity that signs a certificate, thus verifying that the identity contained in that certificate is correct. You should only trust a certificate that has been signed by an authority you trust.

On opening a TLS connection to a particular destination, the client that initiates the connection receives a certificate from the far end, which it can check to make sure that it is talking to the entity that it intended to reach. For example, when you open a web connection to your bank, your browser checks that the certificate matches the URL of your bank, and it also checks what CA signed the certificate.

Other components need to be able to safely identify the CA, so it is represented by a certificate. But that certificate needs to be signed by a CA, and in order to verify the signer's identity, there needs to be need another certificate, and so on and so forth. It seems that we could build a never-ending chain of certificates! Eventually, there has to be a certificate that we can trust.

In practice, the chain ends with what's called a self-signed certificate: an X.509 certificate that the CA signed for itself. In other words, the identity represented by the certificate is the same as the identity whose private key is used to sign the certificate. If you can trust that identity, you can trust the certificate. Figure 11-4 shows a certificate chain, where Ann's certificate is signed by Bob, and Bob's is signed by Carol. The chain ends with Carol's self-signed certificate.

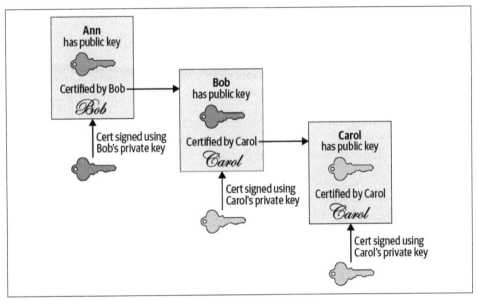

Figure 11-4. Certificate chain

Web browsers come preinstalled with the identities of a set of certificates from well-known, trusted CAs known as root CAs. Your web browser will trust any certificate (or certificate chain) signed by one of these root CAs. If the certificate isn't signed by one of the trusted CAs for the browser, it will show the site as insecure (and in browsers today you will almost certainly see a warning or error message).

If you're setting up a website that people will connect to over the internet, you will need a certificate for that website signed by a trusted, public CA. There are several vendors who act as these CAs and will generate a certificate for a fee, or you can get one for free from Let's Encrypt (*https://letsencrypt.org*).

When you're setting up distributed system components such as, say, Kubernetes or etcd, you get to specify a set of CAs that are used to validate certificates. Assuming that your system is under your private control, it doesn't matter to you whether members of the public at large (or their browsers) trust these components—the important thing is that the components can trust each other. Because this is a private system, you don't need to use publicly trusted CAs, and you can very simply set up your own certificate authorities with self-signed certificates.

Whether you're using your own CA or a public one, you'll need to tell the CA about the certificate(s) you want generated. This is done with a Certificate Signing Request.

Certificate Signing Requests

A Certificate Signing Request (CSR) is a file that includes the following information:

- The public key that the certificate will incorporate
- The domain name(s) that this certificate should work with
- Information about the identity that this certificate should represent (for example, the name of your company or organization)

You create a CSR and send it to a CA to request an X.509 certificate. You know from earlier in the chapter that a certificate includes this information, plus the signature from the CA, so it makes complete sense that this is what is included in a CSR.

Tools like openssl can create a new key pair and CSR in one step. Perhaps confusingly, openssl can take a private key as input for generating a CSR. This makes sense when you recall that the public key is derived from the private key. The component running as this identity (represented by the certificate) will use the private key for decrypting and signing messages (as you'll see shortly), but it never uses the public key itself. It's the other components that it communicates with who will need the public key, and they get that from the certificate. This component needs the private key, and it needs the certificate that it will send to other components.

Now that you have a good understanding of what a certificate is, let's discuss how certificates are used for TLS connections.

TLS Connections

Transport layer connections have to be initiated by a component, and that component is called the client. The entity it is communicating with is called the server. It may well be the case that this client-server relationship is true only at the transport layer, and at higher layers the components could be peers.

A client opens a socket and requests a network connection to the server. For a secure connection, it requests that the server should send back a certificate. As you know from earlier in this chapter, the certificate conveys two very important pieces of information: the identity of the server, and its public key.

The point of this is that the client can check that the server can be trusted. The client checks that the server's certificate was signed by a trusted CA, and if so, that is confirmation that the server can be trusted. The client can go on to use the server's public key to encrypt messages that it sends to the server. The client and server agree on a symmetric key used for the remainder of the messages transferred on this connection —this is more performant than using the asymmetric public/private key pair. This message flow is shown in Figure 11-5.

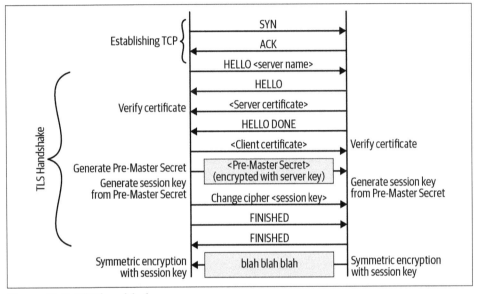

Figure 11-5. TLS handshake

You may have come across the term "skip verify." This refers to an option at the transport layer that allows a client to skip the step where it verifies that the certificate was signed by a known CA. The client simply assumes that the identity claimed by the certificate is correct. This can be handy in nonproduction environments because it means you don't have to bother configuring the client with information about CAs, and you can simply use self-signed certificates. You still have encrypted communications between components, but you can't have full confidence that components aren't imposters, so please don't use skip-verify options in production!

Once the client has verified the server, it can trust it. But how can the server trust the client?

If we were discussing a website where you have an account, like a bank, it's important that the server verifies your identity before it gives out details of your bank balance, or worse. For a true client/server relationship such as logging into your bank, this is typically dealt with through Layer 7 authentication. You supply a username and password, perhaps supplementing this with multi-factor authentication through a code sent in a text message, or through a one-time password generated by a Yubikey, or a mobile app like Authy, 1Password, or Google Auth.

Another way to validate the client's identity is through another X.509 certificate. The message flow in Figure 11-5 shows both the server and client certificates being exchanged—this is an option that can be configured at the server side. The server used one to confirm its identity to the client, so why not do the same thing in reverse? When this happens, it's called mutual TLS or mTLS.

Secure Connections Between Containers

Nothing in this chapter so far is specific to containers, but now let's review some of the circumstances in which you might need to understand keys, certificates, and certificate authorities:

- If you are installing or administering Kubernetes or other distributed system components, it's likely that you'll come across options for using secure connections. Installation tools like kubeadm now make it easy to use TLS between control plane components, automatically configuring certificates as appropriate. This doesn't do anything to secure the traffic between containers and the outside world.

- As a developer, you might write application code that sets up secure connections with other components (whether it's running in a container or not). In that case, your app code needs access to certificates that you'll need to create.

- Rather than writing your own code to set up secure connections, you can choose to use a service mesh to do it for you.

Certificates are intended for distribution, but to use them each component also needs access to its own private key corresponding to that certificate. The next chapter discusses how secret data such as private keys can be passed into containers.

Certificate Revocation

Imagine that an attacker somehow obtains a private key. They can now impersonate the identity associated with that key, because they can successfully decrypt messages that were encrypted using the public key embedded in any corresponding certificates. To prevent this, you need a way of invalidating the certificate immediately, rather than waiting for its expiry date.

This invalidation is called "certificate revocation" and can be achieved by maintaining a Certificate Revocation List (CRL) of certificates that should no longer be accepted.

Try not to share identities (and their certificates) across multiple components or users. It may seem like a management burden to set up individual identities and certificates for each component, but it means you can revoke the certificate for one identity without having to reissue a new one to all the (legitimate) users. It also allows for a separation of concerns whereby each identity can be granted a separate set of permissions.

In Kubernetes, certificates are used by the kubelet component on each node to authenticate to the API server and confirm that it really is an authorized kubelet. These certificates can be rotated (*https://oreil.ly/b0eon*).

Certificates are also one of the mechanisms that clients can use to authenticate themselves with the Kubernetes API Server (*https://oreil.ly/0DuGQ*).

At the time of writing, Kubernetes does not support certificate revocation (*https://oreil.ly/RU3ga*). You can use RBAC configuration to prevent API access for the client associated with that certificate.

Summary

To avoid man-in-the-middle attacks, you'll need to make sure that you can trust the network connections between your various software components. Secure connections based on mTLS are a tried-and-tested way to ensure this is the case. It's a good idea to set up mTLS between your application containers, and if you're administering distributed system components, you will need secure connections between them as well.

Each container or other component using X.509 certificates for authentication will need three things:

- A private key that should never be shared and should be treated as a secret
- A certificate that it can freely distribute, which other components can use to validate its identity
- Certificates from one or more trusted CAs that it can use to validate the certificates received from other components

Now that you have read this chapter, you should have a good understanding of the role that keys, certificates, and CAs each play. This knowledge will be helpful when you're configuring components to use them.

If you can trust the connections between containers and identify the component at the far end of a connection, you are in a good place to start passing *secrets* between containers. But you'll need to be able to pass secret values into containers safely—and that's what's coming up in the next chapter.

Passing Secrets to Containers

Application code often needs certain credentials to do its job. For example, it may need a password to access a database, or a token giving it permission to access a particular API. Credentials, or secrets, exist specifically to restrict access to resources—the database or the API in these examples. It's important to make sure that the secrets themselves stay "secret" and, in compliance with the principle of least privilege, are accessible only to people or components who really need them.

This chapter starts by considering the desirable properties of secrets and then explores the options for getting secret information into containers. It ends with a discussion of native support for secrets in Kubernetes.

Secret Properties

The most obvious property of a secret is that it needs to be secret—that is, it must be accessible only to the people (or things) that are supposed to have access. Typically you ensure this secrecy by encrypting the secret data and sharing the decryption key only with those entities that should have permission to see the secret.

The secret should be stored in encrypted form so that it's not accessible to every user or entity that can access the data store. When the secret moves from storage to wherever it's used, it should also be encrypted so that it can't be sniffed from the network. Ideally, the secret should never be written to disk unencrypted. When the application needs the unencrypted version, it's best if this is held only in memory.

It is perhaps tempting to imagine that once you have encrypted a secret, that is the end of the matter, because you can pass it safely to another component. However, the receiver would need to know how to decrypt the information it received, and that entails a decryption key. This key is in itself a secret, and the receiver would need to get hold of that somehow, leading us back to the original question of how we can pass this next-level secret safely.

You need to be able to *revoke* secrets—that is, make them invalid in the event that the secret should no longer be trusted. This could happen if you know or suspect that an unauthorized person has been able to access the secret. You might also want to revoke secrets for straightforward operational reasons, such as someone leaving the team.

You also want the ability to *rotate* or change secrets. You won't necessarily know if one of your secrets has been compromised, so by changing them every so often you ensure that any attacker who has been able to access some credentials will find that they stop working. It's now well-recognized that forcing humans to change passwords regularly is a bad idea (*https://oreil.ly/ETKEZ*), but software components can cope fine with frequently changing credentials.

The life cycle of a secret should ideally be independent of the life cycle of the component that uses it. This is desirable because it means you don't have to rebuild and redistribute the component when the secret changes.

The set of people who should have access to a secret is often much smaller than the set of people who need access to the application source code that will use that secret, or who can perform deployments or administration on (parts of) the deployment. For example, in a bank, it's unlikely that developers should have access to production secrets that would grant access to account information. It's quite common for secret access to be write-only for humans: once a secret is generated (often automatically and at random), there may never be a reason for a person to legitimately read the secret out again.

It's not just people who should be restricted from having access to secrets. Ideally, the only software components that can read the secret should be those that need access to it. Since we are concerned with containers, this means exposing a secret only to those containers that actually need it to function correctly.

Now that we have considered the preferred qualities of a secret, let's turn to the possible mechanisms that could be used to get a secret into the application code running in a container.

Getting Information into a Container

Bearing in mind that a container is deliberately intended to be an isolated entity, it should be no surprise that there is a limited set of possibilities for getting information —including secret data—into a running container:

- Data can be included in the container image, as a file in the image root filesystem.
- Environment variables can be defined as part of the configuration that goes along with the image (see Chapter 6 for a reminder of how the root filesystem and config information make up an image).
- The container can receive information over a network interface.
- Environment variables can be defined or overridden at the point where the container is run (for example, including -e parameters on a docker run command).
- The container can mount a volume from the host, and read information out of volumes on that host.

Let's take each of these options in turn.

Storing the Secret in the Container Image

The first two of these options are unsuitable for secret data because they require you to hardcode the secret into the image at build time. While this is certainly possible, it is generally considered a bad idea:

- The secret is viewable by anyone who has access to the source code for the image. You might be thinking that the secret could be encrypted rather than in plain text in the source code—but then you'll need to pass in another secret somehow so that the container can decrypt it. What mechanism will you use to pass in this second secret?
- The secret can't change unless you rebuild the container image, but it would be better to decouple these two activities. Furthermore, a centralized, automated system for managing secrets (like CyberArk or Hashicorp Vault) can't control the life cycle of a secret that is hardcoded in the source.

Unfortunately, it is surprisingly common to find secrets baked into source code. One reason is simply that developers don't all know that it's a bad idea; another is that it's all too easy to put the secrets directly into the code as a shortcut during development or testing, with the intention of removing them later—and then simply forget to come back and take them out.

If passing the secret at build time is off the table, the other options all pass the secret when the container starts or is running.

Passing the Secret Over the Network

The third option, passing the secret over a network interface, requires your application code to make the appropriate network calls to retrieve or receive the information, and as a result it is the approach I have seen least often in the wild.

In addition, there is the question of encrypting the network traffic that carries the secret, which necessitates another secret in the form of an X.509 certificate (see Chapter 11). You could offload this part of the problem to a service mesh, which can be configured to ensure that network connections use mutual TLS for security.

Passing Secrets in Environment Variables

The fourth option, passing secrets via environment variables, is generally frowned upon for a couple of reasons:

- In many languages and frameworks, a crash will result in the system dumping debug information that may well include all the environment settings. If this information gets passed to a logging system, anyone who has access to the logs can see secrets passed in as environment variables.

- If you can run docker inspect (or an equivalent) on a container, you get to see any environment variables defined for the container, whether at build or at runtime. Administrators who have good reasons for inspecting properties of a container don't necessarily need access to the secrets.

Here's an example of extracting the environment variables from a container image:

```
vagrant@vagrant:~$ docker image inspect --format '{{.Config.Env}}' nginx
[PATH=/usr/local/sbin:/usr/local/bin:/usr/sbin:/usr/bin:/sbin:/bin NGINX_VERSION=
1.17.6 NJS_VERSION=0.3.7 PKG_RELEASE=1~buster]
```

You can also easily inspect environment variables at runtime. This example shows how the results include any definitions passed in on the run command (EXTRA_ENV here).

```
vagrant@vagrant:~$ docker run -e EXTRA_ENV=HELLO --rm -d nginx
13bcf3c571268f697f1e562a49e8d545d78aae65b0a102d2da78596b655e2f9a
vagrant@vagrant:~$ docker container inspect --format '{{.Config.Env}}' 13bcf
[EXTRA_ENV=HELLO PATH=/usr/local/sbin:/usr/local/bin:/usr/sbin:/usr/bin:/sbin:/bin
NGINX_VERSION=1.17.6 NJS_VERSION=0.3.7 PKG_RELEASE=1~buster]
```

The 12-factor app manifesto (*https://12factor.net/config*) encourages developers to pass configuration through environment variables, so in practice you may find yourself running third-party containers that expect to be configured this way, including some secret values. You can mitigate the risk of environment variable secrets in a few ways (which may or may not be worthwhile, depending on your risk profile):

- You could process output logs to remove or obscure the secret values.

- You can modify the app container (or use a sidecar container) to retrieve the secrets from a secure store (like Hashicorp Vault, CyberArk Conjur, or cloud provider secret/key management systems). Some commercial security solutions will provide this integration for you.

One last thing to note about secrets configured through environment variables is that the environment for a process is configured only once, and that's at the point where the process is created. If you want to rotate a secret, you can't reconfigure the environment for the container from the outside.

Passing Secrets Through Files

The preferred option for passing secrets is to write them into files that the container can access through a mounted volume. Ideally, this mounted volume should be a temporary directory that is held in memory rather than written to disk. Combining this with a secure secrets store ensures that secrets are never stored "at rest" unencrypted.

Because the file is mounted from the host into the container, it can be updated from the host side at any time without having to restart the container. Provided the application knows to retrieve a new secret from the file if the old secret stops working, this means you can rotate secrets without having to restart containers.

Kubernetes Secrets

If you're using Kubernetes, the good news is that it has native secrets support that meets many of the criteria I described at the start of this chapter:

- Kubernetes secrets are created as independent resources, so they are not tied to the life cycle of the application code that needs them.

- Secrets can be encrypted at rest, although (at least as of this writing) you will need to opt in to this as it's *not enabled by default*.

- Secrets are encrypted in transit between components. This requires that you have secure connections between Kubernetes components, though this is generally the case by default in most distributions.

- Kubernetes secrets support the file mechanism as well as the environment variable method, mounting secrets as files in a temporary filesystem that is held in-memory and never written to disk.

- You can set up Kubernetes RBAC (role-based access control) so that users can configure secrets but can't access them again, giving them write-only permissions.

By default in Kubernetes the secret values are stored in the etcd data store as base64-encoded but not encrypted values. It is possible to configure etcd to encrypt its data store, though you will need to take care not to store the decryption key on the host.

In my experience most enterprises choose a third-party commercial solution for secret storage, either from their cloud provider (such as the AWS Key Management System, or its Azure or GCP equivalents), or from a vendor such as Hashicorp or CyberArk. These offer several benefits:

- One reason is certificate rotation. When you rotate the certificates that Kubernetes components themselves use, you will need to refresh all the Kubernetes secrets (*https://oreil.ly/wHHDf*). This can be avoided by using a dedicated secrets management solution.

- Another benefit is that a dedicated secrets management system can be shared with multiple clusters. Secret values can be rotated, irrespective of the life cycle of the application cluster(s).

- These solutions can make it easier for organizations to standardize on one way of handling secrets, with common best practices for management and consistent logs and auditing of secrets.

> The Kubernetes documentation covers many of the security properties (*https://oreil.ly/XmzCc*) of its native secrets support.
>
> Rancher's documentation includes an example of using AWS KMS for Kubernetes secret encryption (*https://oreil.ly/qi6yC*) at rest.
>
> There is also a description of injecting secrets from Vault (*https://oreil.ly/CyN1J*) on Hashicorp's blog.

Secrets Are Accessible by Root

Whether a secret is passed into a container as a mounted file or as an environment variable, it is going to be possible for the root user on the host to access it.

If the secret is held in a file, that file lives on the host's filesystem somewhere. Even if it's in a temporary directory, the root user will be able to access it. As an demonstration of this you can list the temporary filesystems mounted on a Kubernetes node, and you'll find something like this:

```
root@vagrant:/$ mount -t tmpfs
...
tmpfs on /var/lib/kubelet/pods/f02a9901-8214-4751-b157-d2e90bc6a98c/volumes/kuber
netes.io~secret/coredns-token-gxsqd type tmpfs (rw,relatime)
tmpfs on /var/lib/kubelet/pods/074d762f-00ed-48e6-a22f-43fc673df0e6/volumes/kuber
netes.io~secret/kube-proxy-token-bvktc type tmpfs (rw,relatime)
tmpfs on /var/lib/kubelet/pods/e1bad0db-8c0b-4d7b-8867-9fc019de258f/volumes/kuber
netes.io~secret/default-token-h2x8p type tmpfs (rw,relatime)
...
```

Using the directory names included in this output, the root user has no difficulty accessing the secret files held within them.

Extracting the secrets held in environment variables is almost as simple for the root user. Let's demonstrate this by starting a container with Docker on the command line, passing in an environment variable:

```
vagrant@vagrant:~$ docker run --rm -it -e SECRET=mysecret ubuntu sh
$ env
...
SECRET=mysecret
...
```

This container is running sh, and from another terminal you can find the process ID for that executable:

```
vagrant@vagrant:~$ ps -C sh
  PID TTY          TIME CMD
17322 pts/0    00:00:00 sh
```

In Chapter 4 you saw that lots of interesting information about a process is held in the /proc directory. That includes all its environment variables, held in /proc/<pro cess ID>/environ:

```
vagrant@vagrant:~$ sudo cat /proc/17322/environ
PATH=/usr/local/sbin:/usr/local/bin:/usr/sbin:/usr/bin:/sbin:/binHOSTNAME=2cc99c9
8ba5aTERM=xtermSECRET=mysecretHOME=/root
```

As you can see, any secret passed in through the environment can be read in this way. Are you wondering whether it wouldn't be better to encrypt the secret first? Think about how you would get the decryption key—which also needs to be kept secret—into the container.

I can't overemphasize that anyone who has root access to a host machine has carte blanche over everything on that machine, including all its containers and their secrets. This is why it's so important to prevent unauthorized root access within your deployment, and why running as root inside a container is so dangerous: since root inside the container is root on the host, it is just one step away from compromising everything on that host.

Summary

If you have worked through the book to this point, you should have a good understanding of how containers work, and you know how to send secret information safely between them. You have seen numerous ways in which containers can be exploited, and many ways in which they can be protected.

The last group of protection mechanisms we shall consider relates to *runtime protection*, coming up in the next chapter.

Container Runtime Protection

As we saw in Chapter 10, one of the characteristics of containers is they lend themselves to *microservice* architectures. Application developers can break down a complex software application into small, self-contained pieces of code that can be scaled independently, each delivered as a container image.

Breaking a large system into smaller components with well-defined interfaces makes it easier to design, code, and test the individual components. It also turns out to make them easier to secure.

Container Image Profiles

If a given container image holds the code for an application microservice and that microservice does one small function, it's relatively easy to reason about what that microservice should do. The code for the microservice is built into a container image, and it's possible to construct a runtime profile corresponding to that container image, defining what it should be able to do.

Every container instantiated from a given image should behave the same way, so it makes sense that a profile of expected behavior can be defined for an image and then used to police the traffic to and from all the containers based on that image.

 In a Kubernetes deployment, runtime security might be policed on a pod-by-pod basis—for example, through the PodSecurityPolicy object, or through security tools that also act at this level. A pod is essentially a collection of containers that share a network namespace, so the underlying mechanisms for runtime security are the same.

I'll use the same ecommerce platform example from "Container Firewalls" on page 117, with a product search microservice that accepts web requests specifying a search term (or the first few characters of a search term) as entered by a customer browsing the ecommerce site. The job of the product search microservice is to look in a product database for items that match the search term and return a response. Let's start by thinking about the expected network traffic for this microservice.

Network Traffic Profiles

From the description of the product search microservice, we can infer that its containers need to accept and respond to web requests coming from a particular ingress or load balancer, and they should initiate a database connection to the product database. Aside from common platform functions like logging or health checks, there is really no reason for this service to handle or initiate any other network traffic.

It would not be terribly onerous to draw up a profile defining the traffic that is permitting for this service and then use it to define rules that are enforced at the networking level, as you saw in Chapter 10. Some security tools can act in a recording mode in which they monitor messages to and from a service over a period of time to automatically build up a profile of what normal traffic flow looks like. This profile can be converted into container firewall rules or network policies.

Network traffic isn't the only behavior that you can observe and profile. Let's consider the executables.

Executable Profiles

How many executable programs should run in this product search microservice? For the sake of illustration, let's imagine that the code is written as a single Go executable called productsearch. If you were to monitor the executables running inside these product search containers, you should only ever see productsearch. Anything else would be an anomaly and possibly a sign of attack.

Even if the service is written in a scripted language like Python or Ruby, you can make inferences about what is or isn't acceptable. Does the service need to "shell out" to run other commands? If not, then were you ever to observe bash, sh, or zsh executables running in a product search container, you should be alarmed.

This relies on you treating the containers as immutable and assumes that you are not opening shells directly into containers on your production system. From a security perspective, there is very little difference between an attacker opening a reverse shell through an application vulnerability and an administrator opening a shell to perform some kind of "maintenance." As discussed in "Immutable Containers" on page 87, this is considered bad practice!

So how can you spot the executables being launched within a container? One technology for doing this is eBPF.

Observing executables with eBPF

Let's consider an `nginx` container as an example. Under normal circumstances, the only processes you expect to see inside such a container are `nginx` processes. Using the Tracee project that you first met in Chapter 8, I can easily observe the processes that are started inside an `nginx` container.

Tracee uses a technology called eBPF (which stands for extended Berkeley Packet Filter). eBPF lets Tracee insert code into the kernel, so it needs to be run as root.

To delve into eBPF, you might like to start with the slides from my talk on eBPF Superpowers (*https://oreil.ly/-ERmb*). Then you'll find a lot more information and resources on Brendan Gregg's website (*http://brendangregg.com*).

After starting Tracee in one terminal, I run an `nginx` container from another:

```
$ docker run --rm -d --name nginx nginx
```

Tracee shows the `nginx` executable starting up, just as expected (I have omitted some output for clarity):

```
EVENT   ARGS
execve /usr/sbin/nginx
```

Now if I execute another command inside the container—for example, `docker exec -it nginx ls`—the executable shows up in Tracee's output:

```
EVENT   ARGS
execve /usr/sbin/nginx
execve /bin/ls
```

Imagine that, as an attacker, I insert a cryptocurrency miner inside this container. When the miner executable starts, a tool like Tracee can spot the executable. Runtime security tools can carry out this kind of observation, using eBPF or proprietary technology to spot when executables are launched and comparing the executable name against a whitelist or blacklist. I'll come to the shortcomings of today's eBPF-based tooling shortly.

First, let's consider some of the other properties that can be profiled for a given container image.

File Access Profiles

Much as you can use eBPF or other technologies to observe when a system call is used to start an executable, you can observe the system calls that access files. Generally speaking, the set of file locations that you would expect a given microservice to access is also relatively limited. As an example, using Tracee I obtained the following list of files for an nginx container:

```
openat  /etc/ld.so.cache
openat  /lib/x86_64-linux-gnu/libdl.so.2
openat  /lib/x86_64-linux-gnu/libpthread.so.0
openat  /lib/x86_64-linux-gnu/libcrypt.so.1
openat  /lib/x86_64-linux-gnu/libpcre.so.3
openat  /usr/lib/x86_64-linux-gnu/libssl.so.1.1
openat  /usr/lib/x86_64-linux-gnu/libcrypto.so.1.1
openat  /lib/x86_64-linux-gnu/libz.so.1
openat  /lib/x86_64-linux-gnu/libc.so.6
openat  /etc/localtime
openat  /var/log/nginx/error.log
openat  /usr/lib/ssl/openssl.cnf
openat  /sys/devices/system/cpu/online
openat  /etc/nginx/nginx.conf
openat  /etc/nsswitch.conf
openat  /etc/ld.so.cache
openat  /lib/x86_64-linux-gnu/libnss_files.so.2
openat  /etc/passwd
openat  /etc/group
openat  /etc/nginx/mime.types
openat  /etc/nginx/conf.d
openat  /etc/nginx/conf.d/default.conf
openat  /var/log/nginx/error.log
openat  /var/log/nginx/access.log
openat  /var/run/nginx.pid
openat  /proc/sys/kernel/ngroups_max
openat  /etc/group
```

This list is sufficiently long that even an experienced programmer might omit a few of these files if they tried to draw up a profile by hand, but with tools like Tracee it's straightforward to create the list of files that a container is expected to access. Again, some security tools offer the ability to profile running containers automatically and then alert on or prevent opening files outside the expected profile.

User ID Profiles

As discussed in Chapter 6, you can define the user ID under which processes run within a container, so this is another aspect that can be policed by security tools at runtime. (I hope you're using non-root users in your application profiles—see "Containers Run as Root by Default" on page 105.)

As a general rule, if the container is doing one job, it probably needs to operate under only one user identity. If you were to observe the container using a different identity, this would be another red flag. If a process were to be unexpectedly running as root, this privilege escalation would be an even greater cause for concern.

Other Runtime Profiles

You can go to an even lower level and profile `productsearch` to determine the set of system calls and capabilities that it needs to make. From this, you can create a "shrink-wrapped" seccomp or AppArmor profile (see Chapter 8) that applies specifically to the containers running `productsearch`. Jess Frazelle's `bane` (*https://oreil.ly/aQy3Q*) is a tool for generating AppArmor profiles like this.

Using Tracee to observe `cap_capable` system calls, I obtained the following list of capabilities required for the `nginx` container:

```
CAP_CHOWN
CAP_DAC_OVERRIDE
CAP_DAC_READ_SEARCH
CAP_NET_BIND_SERVICE
CAP_SETGID
CAP_SETUID
CAP_SYS_ADMIN
```

A similar exercise would result in a list of system calls used by the container that could be converted into a seccomp profile.

It is much easier to build up this kind of profile for microservice applications than it is for monoliths, because the number of possible paths through a microservice is dramatically smaller. It's relatively easy to exercise the error paths as well as the happy paths to check whether all file access events, system calls, and executables are accounted for.

You have seen that it's possible to build a profile for what "normal" behavior looks like for a microservice, in terms of what executables, user IDs, and network traffic should be expected. There are several tools available that leverage this kind of profile to provide security at runtime.

Container Security Tools

You have already seen some of these tools in earlier chapters:

- Chapter 8 talked about configuring each container to run with its own AppArmor, SELinux, or seccomp profile.
- Network traffic can be policed at runtime using network policy or a service mesh, as described in Chapter 10.

There are additional tools for policing executables, file access, and user IDs at runtime. Most of these are commercial tools, but one open source option is the CNCF project Falco. This observes container behavior using eBPF and triggers alerts when something anomalous happens, such as an unexpected executable being run (as in the earlier example). This approach is a powerful way to detect anomalous behavior, but it does have limitations when it comes to enforcement. This is because eBPF can detect but can't modify system calls. So while this is efficient and powerful for observing and alerting to potential attacks, you need another mechanism in place to actually stop them. Falco can trigger alerts that you can use either to automatically reconfigure the running system or to call for human intervention.

Prevention or alerting

Whichever tool you use for runtime protection, there is one last aspect to consider: what action do you want the tool to take when it finds anomalous behavior? Ideally, you'd like it to prevent the unexpected in the first place—this is what happens when you apply network policies and seccomp/SELinux/AppArmor profiles. But what about the other forms of runtime profiles discussed in this chapter?

Commercial tools that offer true runtime protection use proprietary techniques that hook into the container and can prevent it from running anomalous executables, using an incorrect user ID, or making unexpected file/network access.

Typically, these tools also offer a mode in which anomalous behavior merely triggers an alert rather than taking preventive action. This can be useful during a trial stage to ensure that the runtime profiles are correctly set up.

If you're using a tool that can't prevent out-of-profile behavior, it will provide you with alerts. This means you'll get a notification that a container is behaving badly in some way. How you should handle such alerts is a complicated question:

- If you automatically delete the container when it triggers an alert, will this affect the service for users?
- Furthermore, if you delete the container, will it erase evidence that would be useful for forensics?
- You could terminate just the specific process that triggered the alert, but what if that's a "good" process that has been coerced into doing something unexpected (for example, through an injection attack)?
- If you're relying on an orchestrator to bring up a new instance, what if the new instance is subject to the same attack? You can end up in a vicious cycle in which a container comes up, bad behavior is detected, and the security tool kills the container, only for it to be re-created by the orchestrator (for example, think about how Kubernetes will create or destroy pods to ensure that the number matches the desired replica count).

- If this is a new version of a container, can you roll back to the previous version?
- Should you simply rely on human intervention to investigate the unexpected behavior and determine how to react? This approach inevitably means a significant delay before reacting to the attack, and this delay may be long enough to allow the attack to extract the data or create damage as it was intended to.

There is no single correct answer when it comes to figuring out how to handle a security alert automatically. However long it takes *might* be long enough for an attacker to cause harm. Prevention is much better than cure in this regard.

If your security tools can actually prevent bad behavior within a container before it happens, there is a possibility that the container can carry on as before. For example, suppose an attacker has compromised a product search container and is attempting to run a cryptocurrency miner. The executable is not part of the profile, so the runtime security tool prevents it from being run at all. The "good" processes carry on as normal, but the cryptomining attack is prevented.

The best option is tooling that can prevent anomalous behavior but that generates alerts or logs so you can investigate and determine whether it is a genuine attack and, if so, decide on the appropriate next steps.

Drift Prevention

As you'll recall from "Immutable Containers" on page 87, it's considered best practice to treat your containers as immutable. The container is instantiated from its image, and then the contents of the container should not change. Any executables or dependencies that the application code needs should be included in that image. We discussed this earlier through the lens of vulnerability detection: you can't scan for vulnerabilities in code that isn't included in the image, so you should make sure that everything you want to scan is included.

Treating containers as immutable gives us another incredibly powerful option for detecting code injection at runtime: *drift prevention*, which should be offered by any serious runtime security solution for containers. This requires coordination between the scanning and runtime steps:

- The scanner fingerprints the files within the image as part of the scan.
- At runtime, an enforcement tool adds a check whenever a container starts to run a new executable process. This enforcer compares the executable against the file fingerprints from the scanning step. If the file isn't identical, the executable is not permitted to run (giving a "permission denied" error within the container).

By using file fingerprints rather than a list of filenames, this approach can prevent an attacker from trying to disguise an injected executable as a legitimate one.

Summary

The ability to do granular runtime protection, as described in this chapter, makes specialist container security tooling a compelling prospect, especially for organizations with a lot at risk, such as banks or healthcare organizations.

You're closing in on the end of the book now. The final chapter reviews the top 10 security risks collated by OWASP and relates these risks to mitigations that are specific to containerized deployments.

CHAPTER 14

Containers and the OWASP Top 10

If you're in the security field, there's a good chance you have come across OWASP (*https://owasp.org*), the Open Web Application Security Project; perhaps you're even a member of a local chapter. This organization periodically publishes a list of the top 10 web application security risks.

While not all applications, containerized or otherwise, are web applications, this is a great resource for considering which attacks to be most concerned about. You'll also find great explanations of these attacks and advice on how to prevent them on the OWASP website. In this chapter, I'll relate the current top 10 risks (*https://owasp.org/ www-project-top-ten*) to container-specific security approaches.

Injection

If your code has an injection flaw, an attacker can get it to execute commands masquerading as data. This is perhaps best illustrated through the immortal *xkcd* character Little Bobby Tables (*https://xkcd.com/327*).

There is nothing container-specific about this, though container image scanning can reveal known injection vulnerabilities in dependencies. You should review and test your own application code, following the OWASP advice.

Broken Authentication

This category covers broken authentication and compromised credentials. At the application level, all the same advice applies for containerized apps as for monoliths in traditional deployments, but there are some additional container-specific considerations:

- The credentials required by each container should be treated as secrets. These secrets need to be stored with care and passed into containers at runtime, as discussed in Chapter 12.

- Breaking an application into multiple containerized components means that they need to identify each other, typically using certificates, and communicate using secure connections. This can be handled directly by containers, or you can use a service mesh to offload this responsibility. See Chapter 11.

Sensitive Data Exposure

It is particularly important to protect any personal, financial, or other sensitive data that your application has access to.

Whether containerized or not, sensitive information should always be encrypted at rest and in transit, using a strong cryptographic algorithm. Over time, as processing power increases, it becomes feasible to brute-force encryption, which means that older algorithms can start to be considered no longer safe to use.

Because the sensitive data is encrypted, your applications will need credentials to access it. Following the principles of least privilege and segregation of duties, limit credentials to only those containers that really need access. See Chapter 12 for coverage of safely passing secrets to containers.

Consider scanning container images for embedded keys, passwords, and other sensitive data.

XML External Entities

There is nothing container-specific about this category of vulnerable XML processors. Much as for injection vulnerabilities, you should follow the OWASP advice on analyzing your own application code for flaws and use a container image scanner to spot vulnerabilities in dependencies.

Broken Access Control

This category relates to the abuse of privileges that may be granted unnecessarily to users or components. There are some container-specific approaches to applying least privilege to containers, as discussed in Chapter 9:

- Don't run containers as root.
- Limit the capabilities granted to each container.
- Use seccomp, AppArmor, or SELinux.

- Use rootless containers, if possible.

These approaches can limit the blast radius of an attack, but none of these controls relate to user privileges *at the application level,* so you should still apply all the same advice as you would in a traditional deployment.

Security Misconfiguration

Many attacks take advantage of systems that are poorly configured. Examples highlighted in the OWASP Top 10 include insecure or incomplete configurations, open cloud storage, and verbose error messages containing sensitive information, all of which have mitigations specific to containers and cloud native deployments:

- Use guidelines like the Center for Internet Security (CIS) Benchmarks to assess whether your system is configured according to best practices. There are benchmarks for Docker and Kubernetes, as well as for the underlying Linux host. It may not be appropriate in your environment to follow every recommendation, but they are a very good starting point for assessing your installation.

- If you are using a public cloud service, there are tools such as CloudSploit (*https://cloudsploit.com*) or DivvyCloud (*https://divvycloud.com*) to check your settings and look for things like publicly accessible storage buckets or poor password policies. Gartner refers to these checks as Cloud Security Posture Management (CSPM). (Full disclosure: CloudSploit is operated by my employer, Aqua Security.)

- As discussed in Chapter 12, using environment variables to convey secrets can easily result in them being exposed via logs, so I encourage you to use environment variables only for information that isn't sensitive.

You might also want to consider the configuration information that forms part of each container image under this OWASP category. This was covered in Chapter 6, along with best practices for building images securely.

Cross-Site Scripting XSS

This is another category that acts at the application level, so there is nothing particular about running your app in containers that would affect this risk. You should use a container image scanner to identify vulnerable dependencies.

Insecure Deserialization

In this type of attack, a malicious user provides a crafted object that the application interprets to grant the user additional privileges or to change the application behavior in some way. (I witnessed an example of this myself back in 2011 as a Citibank customer, when Citi had a vulnerability (*https://oreil.ly/EsgO7*) allowing a logged-in user to access other people's accounts simply by modifying the URL.)

Again, this is generally not something that is affected by whether an application is running in containers or not, though there are some container-specific approaches to limiting the impact of this kind of attack:

- The OWASP advice on prevention includes a recommendation to isolate the code that performs deserializing and run it in a low-privilege environment. Performing that deserialization step in a dedicated container microservice could provide that isolation, especially if using Firecracker, gVisor, Unikernels, or other approaches that we saw in Chapter 8. Running the container as non-root, with as few capabilities as possible and with a shrink-wrapped seccomp/AppArmor/SELinux profile, would also help limit the privileges that this kind of attack could try to leverage.

- Another recommendation from OWASP here is to restrict network traffic to and from the containers or servers that deserialize. You have seen approaches for restricting network traffic in Chapter 10.

Using Components with Known Vulnerabilities

I hope that by this stage in the book you can anticipate my advice on this: use an image scanner to identify known vulnerabilities in your container images. You also need a process or tooling in place to:

- Rebuild container images to use up-to-date, fixed packages
- Identify and replace running containers based on vulnerable images

Insufficient Logging and Monitoring

The OWASP site shares the terrifying statistic that, on average, breaches take almost 200 days to be identified. It should be possible to dramatically reduce that with sufficient observation combined with alerting on unexpected behavior.

In any production deployment, you should be logging container events, including:

- Container start/stop events, including the identity of the image and the invoking user
- Access to secrets
- Any modification of privileges

- Modification of container payload, which could indicate code injection (see "Drift Prevention" on page 155)
- Inbound and outbound network connections
- Volume mounts (for analysis of mounts that might subsequently turn out to be sensitive, as described in "Mounting Sensitive Directories" on page 113)
- Failed actions such as attempts to open network connections, write to files, or change user permissions, as these could indicate an attacker performing reconnaissance on the system

Most serious commercial container security tools integrate with enterprise SIEM (security information and event management) to provide container security insights and alerts through one centralized system. Even better than observing attacks and reporting on them after the event, these tools can provide the protection of not just reporting on unexpected behaviors but preventing them from happening based on runtime profiles, as discussed in Chapter 13.

Summary

The OWASP Top 10 is a useful resource for making any internet-connected application more secure against the most common types of attack.

You may have spotted that the container-specific recommendation that comes up most often in this chapter is to scan container images for known vulnerabilities in third-party dependencies. While it will fail to catch some things (in particular, exploitable flaws in your own application code), this will probably give you the biggest bang per buck of any preventative tool that you can introduce into a containerized deployment.

Conclusions

Congratulations on reaching the end of this book!

My first hope for you at this point is that you now have a solid mental model of what containers are. This will serve you well in discussions about how to secure your container deployments. You should also be armed with knowledge about different isolation options, should regular containers not give you enough isolation between workloads for your environment.

I also hope that you now have a good understanding of how containers communicate with each other and the outside world. Networking is a vast topic in its own right, but the most important takeaway here is that containers give you a unit not just of deployment but also of security. There are lots of options for restricting traffic so that only what is expected can flow between containers and to/from the outside world.

I'd imagine that you see how layered defenses will serve you well in the event of a breach. If an attacker takes advantage of a vulnerability in your deployment, there are still other walls they may not be able to breach. The more layers of defense, the less likely an attack is to succeed.

As you saw in Chapter 14, there are some preventative measures unique to containers that you can apply against the most commonly exploited attacks against web applications. That top 10 list doesn't cover all the possible weaknesses in your deployment. Now that you have almost reached the end of the book, you might want to review the list of attack vectors specific to containers in "Container Threat Model" on page 3. You will also find a list of questions in the Appendix to help you assess where your deployment might be most vulnerable and where you should beef up your defenses.

I hope that the information in this book helps you to defend your deployment, come what may. If you are subject to an attack—whether you are breached or you succeed in keeping your application and data safe—I would love to hear about it. Feedback, comments, and stories about attacks are always welcome, and you can raise issues at *containersecurity.tech*. I'm @lizrice on Twitter (*https://twitter.com/lizrice*).

Security Checklist

This appendix covers some important items you should at least think about when considering how best to secure your container deployments. In your environment it might well not make sense to apply *every* item, but if you have thought about them, you will be off to a good start. No doubt this list is not absolutely comprehensive!

- Are you running all containers as a non-root user? See "Containers Run as Root by Default" on page 105.

- Are you running any containers with the `--privileged` flag? Are you dropping capabilities that aren't needed for each image? See "The --privileged Flag and Capabilities" on page 111.

- Are you running containers as read-only where possible? See "Immutable Containers" on page 87.

- Are you checking for sensitive directories mounted from the host? How about the Docker socket? See "Mounting Sensitive Directories" on page 113 and "Mounting the Docker Socket" on page 114.

- Are you running your CI/CD pipeline in your production cluster? Does it have privileged access or use the Docker socket? See "The Dangers of docker build" on page 68.

- Are you scanning your container images for vulnerabilities? Do you have a process or tooling in place for rebuilding and redeploying containers where the image is found to include vulnerabilities? See Chapter 7.

- Are you using a seccomp or AppArmor profile? The default Docker profiles are a good starting point; even better would be to shrink-wrap a profile for each application. See Chapter 8.

- If your host operating system supports SELinux, is it enabled? Do your applications have the right SELinux profiles attached? See "SELinux" on page 98.

- What base image are you using? Can you use an option such as a scratch or distroless image, Alpine, or RHEL minimal? Can you minimize the contents of your images to reduce the attack surface? See "Dockerfile Best Practices for Security" on page 75.

- Are you enforcing the use of immutable containers? That is to say, are you making sure that all executable code is added to a container image at build time and not installed at runtime? See "Immutable Containers" on page 87.

- Are you setting resource limits on your containers? See "Setting Resource Limits" on page 26.

- Do you have admission control to make sure that only approved images can be instantiated in production? See "Admission Control" on page 79.

- Are you using mTLS connections between components? This could be implemented within your application code or by using a service mesh. See Chapter 11.

- Do you have a network policy restricting traffic between components? See Chapter 10.

- Are you passing secrets into containers using a temporary filesystem? Are your secrets encrypted at rest and in transit? Are you using a secrets management system for storage and rotation? See Chapter 12.

- Are you using a runtime protection tool to ensure that only expected executables are running inside containers? See Chapter 13.

- Do you have a runtime security solution for drift prevention? See "Drift Prevention" on page 155.

- Are you using hosts exclusively for running containers, separate from other applications? Are you keeping your hosts systems up to date with the latest security releases? Consider running an OS specifically designed for container hosts. See "Container Host Machines" on page 52.

- Are you running regular checks on the security settings on the underlying cloud infrastructure using a CSPM tool? Are your hosts and container configured according to security best practices such as the CIS Benchmarks for Linux, Docker, and Kubernetes? See "Security Misconfiguration" on page 159.

Index

Bazel, 69
Berkeley Packet Filters (BPF) (see BPF)
best practices
    CIS guidelines, 53, 159, 166
    Dockerfile, 75-77
    network policy, 128
/bin directory, 39, 76, 114
binary translation, 60
bind mount, 42, 43
bind package, 90
BIOS (Basic Input Output System), 55
Bitnami, 108
blast radius, limiting, 11, 130, 159
blobs, storing images, 72
booting up
    physical machines, 55
    virtual machines, 57-59
boundaries
    about, 6
    containers as, 11, 31, 53
    sandboxing with gVisor, 102
    Virtual Machine Monitor and, 57
    virtual machines as, 55
BPF (Berkeley Packet Filters), 96
bridge, 120
build command, 68-71
buildah, 69
building
    building new images for updates, 86, 160
    daemonless, 69, 77
    in Docker, 65, 68-71
    within a Kubernetes cluster, 69
    multi-stage, 75
    scanning on, 88, 92
    on separate machines, 77
    vulnerabilities, 4, 74-77
BuildKit, 69

C

cannot fork error, 35
capabilities
    namespaces, 111
    non-root users, 22
    OWASP Top 10, 158
    ping and, 17, 20
    --privileged flag, 111-113, 116, 165
    rootless containers and, 110
    runtime profiles, 153
    setting, 18, 21, 158

tracing, 113
understanding, 19-21
user namespaces, 47, 47, 48
viewing assigned, 20
Capital One, 76
capsh, 47, 112
CAP_NET_ADMIN, 130
CAP_NET_BIND_SERVICE, 19, 48, 110
CAP_NET_RAW, 20
CAP_SETFCAP, 21
CAP_SYS_BOOT, 19
CAP_SYS_MODULE, 19
Center for Internet Security (CIS) (see CIS)
certificate authorities, 132, 134-137, 139
Certificate Signing Request (CSR) (see CSR)
certificates
    certificate authorities, 132, 134-137, 139
    expiration, 133
    generating, 132, 135
    revoking, 138
    rotating, 139, 146
    self-signed, 135
    verifying by browser, 132
    verifying, skipping, 137
    X.509, 132-139, 144
cgroup-tools package, 25
cgroups, 23-30
    about, 53
    configuration, 27
    constraining in image configuration, 68
    controllers, 23, 29
    creating, 24-26, 28, 166
    Docker and, 28
    hierarchies, 23, 26
    listing, 24
    namespaces, 32, 49
    processes, assigning, 27
    V2, 29
Chaubey, Nirbhay, 62
checklist, security, 165
Chiang, Eric, 112
chown, 14
chroot, 38-43
CI/CD (continuous integration/continuous
    development)
    building and storing images, 87, 88, 165
    mounting Docker socket, 114
    --privileged flag, 165
    scanning, 91-93

CVE (Common Vulnerabilities and Exposures), 84

CVE Numbering Authorities (CNAs) (see CNAs)

CVE-2014-6271 (Shellshock), 83, 84, 90

CVE-2018-18955, 47

CVE-2019-5736, 31

CyberArk, 143, 145, 146

D

DAC (discretionary access control), 15-19, 99

data, passing into containers, 142-145, 145
(see also sensitive data)

Debian, 90

decryption (see encryption)

defense in depth principle, 11, 118, 129

delete_module, 96

dependency vulnerabilities, 85, 88, 161

deploying
admission control, 73
images, 78-80
preventing, 93

deserialization, 159

digests, image, 72, 75, 79

Dirty COW, 100

disclosures, responsible security, 83

discretionary access control (DAC) (see DAC)

distroless, 75

DivvyCloud, 159

DNS (Domain Name Service), 78, 119, 120

Docker
about, 1
AppArmor profile, 98, 99
best practices guidelines, 53, 159, 166
building images, 65, 68-71
cgroups and, 28
configuration, overriding, 66
configuration, viewing, 65, 67
daemon, 68, 114
daemonless builds, 69, 77
group, 110
image digest, viewing, 72
on Mac/Windows, 28
mounting Docker socket, 114
networks, setting up multiple, 122
OCI standards, 66
overriding user ID, 107
--privileged flag, 111-113, 116, 165
rootless mode, 68, 111

running containers, xii
running containers as read-only, 109
running containers as root, 106
running containers with no new privileges flag, 19
running containers, overriding root, 66, 76, 107, 110
seccomp, 96, 99
SELinux and, 99
user namespaces in, 46, 48

docker command, xii

Docker Hub registry, 71-73

Docker Trusted Registry, 89

Dockerfile
access control, 74
best practices, 75-77
commands, 65
image layers, 69-71

docs subpackage of bind, 90

domain name
Certificate Signing Request, 136
in certificates, 133
isolating, 32-35
OSI networking model, 119

Domain Name Resolution, 119

Domain Name Service (DNS) (see DNS)

drift prevention, 88, 155, 166

duties, segregation of (see segregation of duties)

E

eBPF (extended Berkeley Packet Filters), 97, 151-153, 154

egress, denying as default, 128

Elastic Container Registry, 71

encryption
Certificate Signing Requests, 136
public/private keys, 133, 141
resources on, 133
secrets, 141, 145, 158, 166
secure connections, 132
sensitive data, 158

ENV (Docker command), 65

environment variables
extracting, 144
overriding, 66
secrets in, 143-145, 147, 159

Envoy, 129

errors
cannot fork error, 35

ITU (International Telecommunications Union), 132

J
Jenkins, 114
JFrog, 89
Justicz, Max, 102

K
Kaniko, 69
Kata Containers, 102
kernel
   checking version of, 49
   initialization, 56
   isolation in, 61
   kernel-level privileges, 13, 56
   memory management, 56, 61
   OSI networking model, 119
Kernel-based Virtual Machines (KVM) (see KVM)
keyctl, 96
keys
   asymmetric, 137
   Certificate Signing Request, 136
   encryption, 133, 141
   generating tools, 132
   scanning, 158
   symmetric, 137
   TLS connections, 137
   X.509 certificates, 132-139
Kritis, 93
kube-proxy, 123, 125
kubeadm, 138
kubelet, 139
Kubernetes, xii
   (see also network policies; orchestrators)
   about, xi, 1
   admission control, 79, 93
   AppArmor and, 98
   best practices guidelines, 53, 159, 166
   certificates for TLS connections, 138, 139
   image configuration, overriding, 66
   image policy, 79
   images, building within a cluster, 69
   interface, xii
   IP addresses in, 121
   iptables, 123-127
   load balancing, 123, 125
   mounting sensitive directories, 114

namespaces, 9
Open Policy Agent, 93
performance, 125
resources on, xii, 146
role-based access control (RBAC), 3, 9
running containers, xii
running containers as read-only, 109
running containers as root, 109
runtime security, 149
seccomp, 96
secrets, 145
service meshes, 129
services, 122, 123
user namespaces support, 46
Kubernetes API Server authentication, 139
Kubernetes Attack Tree, 6
Kubernetes Security (Hausenblas), xii
Kubernetes Threat Model, 6
KVM (Kernel-based Virtual Machines), 59

L
labels, SELinux permissions, 99
languages, compiled, 85
libraries, vulnerabilities in, 85, 88, 161
limiting the blast radius, 11, 130, 159
Linkerd, 129
Linux, xii
   (see also Alpine Linux; capabilities; file permissions; LSM)
   best practices guidelines, 53
   checking version of, 49
   file permissions, 14-19, 98
   namespaces in, 9
   SELinux, 153, 158, 160, 166
   setup for this book, xii
   system calls, 13
   system containers, ix
   Thin OS distributions, 52
   Ubuntu, xii, 25, 40, 49, 84, 90
Linux security modules (LSM) (see LSM)
Little Bobby Tables, 157
load balancing, 123, 125
logging
   best practices, 160
   mounting /log directory, 114
   observability sidecars, 116
   passing secrets to containers and, 144, 159, 160
   policy violations, 98, 99

About the Author

Liz Rice is Chief Open Source Officer at Isovalent, the eBPF and network security specialists behind the Cilium project. Previously, she was Vice President of Open Source Engineering with Aqua Security, where she looked after cloud native security projects including Trivy, Tracee, kube-hunter, and kube-bench. She is chair of CNCF's Technical Oversight Committee and was cochair of the KubeCon + CloudNativeCon 2018 events in Copenhagen, Shanghai, and Seattle.

She has a wealth of software development, team, and product management experience from working on network protocols and distributed systems, and in digital technology sectors such as VOD, music, and VoIP. When not writing code or talking about it, Liz loves riding bikes in places with better weather than her native London, and competing in virtual races on Zwift.

Colophon

The animal on the cover of *Container Security* is an armoured catfish (family *Loricariidae*), also called loricariids, suckermouth catfish, or "plecos" after the species *Hypostomus plecostomus*. These fish are native to Costa Rica, Panama, and South America, where they inhabit freshwater streams and rivers. Armoured catfish are highly adaptable and can flourish in a number of different environments: slow- and fast-moving currents, canals, ponds, lakes, estuaries, and even home aquariums.

There are more than 680 species of loricariids, all of which vary in color, shape, and size. Common traits include the flexible bony plates that distinguish them from other catfish, a flattened body, and a ventral suckermouth that allows these fish to feed, breathe, and attach themselves to various surfaces. The mouth and lips allow for suction and respiration simultaneously, and their bodies and fins are covered in taste buds. They can grow anywhere from three inches to over three feet, depending on conditions. Armoured catfish will eat any number of things, including algae, invertebrates, small bivalves, water fleas, worms, insect larvae, and detritus—one genus, *Panaque*, is known for eating wood. Parental care is common in loricariids and many species will create long burrows along a shoreline where the female will deposit her eggs. Males guard the eggs until they hatch.

Armoured catfish are nocturnal and non-migratory, but they do have a tendency to disperse and potentially displace native fish populations when introduced to a new environment. In addition to their armoured bodies and overall hardiness, armoured catfish have also evolved modified digestive systems that can function as additional respiratory organs. If necessary, these fish can breathe air and survive out of water for more than 20 hours!

The cover illustration is by Karen Montgomery, based on a black-and-white engraving from *Shaw's Zoology*. The cover fonts are Gilroy Semibold and Guardian Sans. The text font is Adobe Minion Pro; the heading font is Adobe Myriad Condensed; and the code font is Dalton Maag's Ubuntu Mono.

O'REILLY®

There's much more where this came from.

Experience books, videos, live online training courses, and more from O'Reilly and our 200+ partners—all in one place.

Learn more at oreilly.com/online-learning

9 781492 056706